A Field Guide to the Urban Hipster

Broadway Books
NEW YORK

A Field Guide to the

Urban Hipster

Josh Aiello

with illustrations by Matthew Shultz

PRINTED IN THE UNITED STATES OF AMERICA

BROADWAY BOOKS and its logo, a letter B bisected on the diagonal, are trademarks of Random House, Inc.

Visit our website at www.broadwaybooks.com

First edition published 2003.

Book design by Gretchen Achilles
Illustrated by Matthew Shultz

The cataloging-in-publication data is on file with the Library of Congress.

ISBN 0-7679-1372-8

10   9   8   7   6   5   4   3   2   1

FOR SUSAN

A Quick Note from the Author

As my request for a travel budget was met with shocked bemusement, the Habitat sections of the following entries are based largely on the comments and opinions of far-flung friends and are the result of several lonely months spent embroiled in online research. The quoted material is not to be taken literally, which should be obvious to anyone with even a cursory understanding of the humor genre. If someone does manage to take offense, the author recommends they write their own book, perhaps on the subject of kittens or daisies.

Contents

Foreword

A Field Guide to the Urban Hipster provides a collection whose breadth is not merely unparalleled in its own field, but perhaps in all of the modern sciences. Social anthropologists such as myself have long anticipated the arrival of Aiello's latest tome. As expected, it is a testament to a brilliant and secretive life's work and the first real stepping-stone for observational hipthologists, both professional and hobbyist.

In May 1989, while still a graduate student at Temple University in Philadelphia, I became vaguely aware of a rapidly gestating group of newly identified specimens. Since classified as "Grunge" (and now largely extinct), all that was known at the time was that these Hipsters subsisted on little more than depressing lyrics, flannel, and an encyclopedic knowledge of trivial pop culture marginalia. In desperate need of a thesis topic, I decided to take a chance.

I soon hit the Seattle streets. If environmental immersion truly is the key to understanding our Hipsters, this remote terrain's possibility of providing meaningful observation seemed elevated. Adjacent to one particular Salvation Army (a well-documented haven for these creatures), I noticed a small coffee shop, Java'Tude. Hoping to gather my notes, I stumbled in. As the barista poured me a mug of the House blend (which I expensed), I noticed a man preparing a latte not six feet away, furtively studying the room from behind the steamer—it was Josh Aiello.

Several summers earlier, Aiello had been my lab partner at a symposium hosted by Boston University. Though we had earned high marks for our joint, evidentiary defense of the rising stigma directed at the Preppie, the symposium's board chair found Aiello's renegade, qualitative methods deplorable. The harshness of this veritable dinosaur's response only reaffirmed my belief that Aiello's work was truly visionary.

Later that fateful Seattle night, Aiello and I met incognito in an effort to preserve his local anonymity. He had recently uncovered a thoroughly peaceful community of coexisting species, most notably the Grungesters and Literati. I sat transfixed as he described his inspired field tactics, a combination of Goodall and grandfather.

By 1990, as the harmony between these northwestern specimens began to unravel, Aiello was dependably one step ahead, warning of the ersatz façade of accord. His *Mopier than Thou*, published in the rainy summer of 1991, analyzed the insidious and subversive turf war for supremacy soon to undermine Genus X. Later, when the beaneries went corporate and Grunge lost its Elvis, the paper's foresight became all too apparent.

And then he vanished. A decade slipped by, during which academia, abandoning much of its hope for a second book, found refuge in the worn bindings of his watershed thesis, *Individuality by the Wayside: "Susie" Pierces Her Navel*. So, when my doorbell rang that night last autumn, I assumed it was my thirty-eight-year-old paper "boy" collecting. But there, using my Sunday *New York Times* as a doormat, stood Dr. Aiello, sopping wet and toting a handwritten copy of *this* book in his satchel.

We settled in before the fire. Aiello, handsome as ever, sipped his brandy and proceeded to tell me where he had been and what he had seen . . .

—WILLIAM GRIFFITH, PH.D.

Professor Emeritus, California State University System, Hipthology

Introduction

I can remember the first time. In the middle school hallway, between periods, as my own sequestered "top-track" English class snaked its way toward History. There was a point where two hallways happened to merge, and it was at this intersection, bottlenecked, practically clinging to the wall, my fingernails digging into my Lamborghini-themed Trapper Keeper, that I caught my first glimpse.

He came stumbling out of art class. Green army jacket. Boots. And there, no more than ten feet away from me, it stood: a perfect blond Mohawk. Right here in South Jersey. Spellbound, I watched as this creature glided effortlessly down the hallway, no doubt on his way to some smoking break or weekly appointment with the guidance counselor. Carefree, without a thought or worry in the world. I stood there quivering.

The days that followed were more confusing than the time my friend Chris doubted his sexuality. I simply could not remove the Mohawk from my consciousness. Was he part Native American? Could he still wear a hat? What did his parents think? How did he decorate his bedroom? Did someone shave the hair for him, or did he do it himself? Did the feat require two mirrors? An electric razor? Would such an act require more coordination than, say, swishing a shot from half court, or less? How much time passes, precisely, from the moment he wakes up to the moment he realizes, "Oh yeah, I have a Mohawk"?

I was dying to confront him. Unfortunately, my overwhelming timidity and rigorous academic schedule forbade such a possibility. Besides, if I were really going to work up the kind of nerve necessary to execute such a gambit, it would surely be in the service of asking Karen Sloan for a dance at Friday evening's dreaded Valentine's event. Moreover, I had been on occasion privy to this pre-shorn personality's penchants for violence and irrationality. Once I had seen him kick (kick!)

someone in the head. Another time I watched from a distance as he drank a can of wood stain in shop class while daring our hapless instructor to stop him. I'm not joking.

So began my affinity for sliding into the shadows. I started tailing him, listening from the next stall, "absentmindedly" falling into the free lunch line behind him, feigning bewilderment at my own sudden enrollment in the music elective. All the while jotting notes, hastily, crudely, my wrist sore from exertion. I could not satiate my curiosity. Who were these Dead Kennedys? Did the correct execution of an anarchy symbol require the use of a protractor? Did these guys love *Webster* as much as I did?

My consumption of Hipster culture soon knew no bounds. I wanted to immerse myself in the peculiarities of their day-to-day existence, to observe as they dyed each other's hair, wondering all the while what they had once been, and who. There was a period, before I became married to my work, when I even became emotionally attached to a specimen or two. I should have known that such things are not meant to be. But I was younger then, and foolish. I even had a goatee.

JAA, BURNING MAN

August 2003

How to Use This Book

Novices in the field study of Urban Hipsters should begin by familiarizing themselves with the illustrations; even the briefest examination of the plates is sufficient to give the beginner an idea of the shapes of our Hipsters and the groups to which they belong. Punks, it will be seen, do not resemble Mods; and Metal Heads are readily separable from Euro Trash. The white face makeup preferred by Goths will immediately distinguish them from the pimply slime exhibited by Internet Geeks. Hipsters of a kind—that is, Hipsters that could be confused—are grouped together herein to allow easy comparison. Thus, when a Hipster has been spotted in the field, the observer can immediately turn to the picture most resembling it and feel confident that he has reduced the possibilities to a few species in its own group.

In many cases, the pictures will suffice without the text. This is true of such easily recognized species as Hippies and Outlaw Bikers. The plates give visual field marks for sorting out species in life. The text supplies field marks such as range, habits, conversational tics, etc., that cannot be pictured.

In cases where the plates, without the text, do not give definitive identifications, the observer should select the illustration most resembling the Hipster he saw, and then consult the appropriate text. We may, for example, be confused by the similarly shaded pink of two otherwise disparately featured Hipsters' hair. By consulting the text entries for both Punks and AlternaGirls, the observer will ultimately conclude that the formfitting Ween T-shirt identifies the specimen as belonging to the latter species. When coupled with the fact that the female Hipster in question, though slightly countercultural, would not be entirely disapproved of by, say, one's conservative Jewish mother, it is clear that this Hipster is no Punk, regardless of plumage.

Far from merely aiding a beginner who can scarcely tell the difference between an Indie Rocker and an Ex-Frat, the advanced student will find this guide comprehensible enough to be of service in recognizing those accidentals or rarities that sometimes appear in the territory he knows so thoroughly.

The *Audiophylum* Family

FIVE SPECIES:

1. GLAM ROCKERS

2. GOTHS

3. METAL HEADS

4. RUDE BOYS (AND GIRLS)

5. THUGZ

Constituting a relatively large and sprawling family, these Hipsters are traditionally grouped together due to their proclivity to assume motifs associated with some musical form. It is important to note, however, that most specimens are thus categorized based merely on appreciation. That is, while some may in fact entertain or perform, they are not distinguished by creativity.

GLAM ROCKERS

ANDROGYNUM FANTASTICA

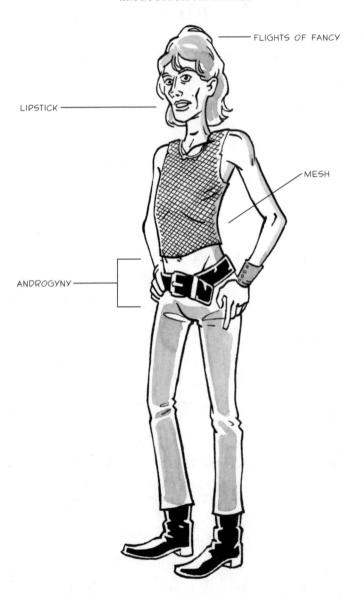

FLIGHTS OF FANCY

LIPSTICK

MESH

ANDROGYNY

GLAM ROCKERS

Male
EXTERIOR: Thin; wiry. Tight pants; sleeveless T-shirt.
MARKINGS: Heavy, shimmery makeup (eyeliner, eye shadow, lip gloss).
PLUMAGE: Spiky.
MOVEMENT: Ornate and theatrical.
VOICE: Syrupy, with affected intonation.

Female [rare, not pictured]
EXTERIOR: Thin, attractive, and boyish; prepubescent. Tight, fashionable clothing.

Noted for their flamboyant, tarted-up appearance, Glam Rockers are perhaps the friendliest and least judgmental of all Hipsters. As such, they invite no known specific natural enemy, though, like many artistic or sexually ambiguous breeds, often suffer general derision ("Fags!") at the hands of most male *Graecus* species [*see*, especially, Ex-Frats].

These Hipsters are, at present, quite rare. In fact, most casual observers respond to the very mention of Glam Rockers with an astounded "They still exist?" They do, though much of their minuscule natural environment was recently further depleted through the concerted effort of the New York City political establishment [e.g., the raids on Coney Island High and Life]. While not targeting Glam Rockers per se, these crackdowns diminished the visibility of the general art scene with which they are associated. Though the ecological rape of their habitat has removed the species from much of public view, small pockets of these Hipsters do remain alive in the wild [*see* Habitat, below]. As endangered, they present quite a challenge to observers.

While much of the species' culture centers around dated music, fashion, and iconography, periodic blips on the pop radar screen have served to keep the scene somewhat fresh [e.g., *Velvet Goldmine, Hedwig and the Angry Inch,* the Toilet Boys, et al.].

Sexual Identity; Orientation:

Glam Rockers, particularly males, present a look of absolute androgyny. As with most aspects of the scene, said androgyny is modeled after an ideal of the 1970s [e.g., David Bowie ca. *Ziggy Stardust*, New York Dolls, et al.], as opposed to the Glam Rock aesthetic of the 1980s, during which makeup was worn by obviously straight, otherwise masculine males [e.g., Poison]. Today, many male Glam Rockers are homosexual, bisexual, or sexually ambiguous.

Mating Habits:

When mating, Glam Rockers tend to stick to their own kind. Coupled boys look strikingly similar to one another, making observation doubly fruitful. In addition, Glam Rockers are never spotted alone; they move only in pairs (same sex or mixed).

While certainly homoerotic, the species is not exclusively homosexual. Male specimens do attract females, who remain undeterred by the male's possible preference for Hipsters of his own gender. Glam Rock Girls function in the scene as equals and are, genitalia aside, exact counterparts of the males—thin, attractive, and fashionable; their androgyny takes the form of prepubescent boyishness.

By Day/By Night:

Glam Rockers are nocturnal creatures. Most pass through the sunlight hours in a substance-induced state of perfect sleepiness, rising in time to report for the night jobs [e.g., musicians, club workers, wait staff, go-go dancers] that fund their drug habits (cocaine, etc.), their socializing (alcohol, condoms), and their expenses (rent, makeup, glitter). Certain Hipsters do venture out-of-doors during daylight hours. Such specimens shed their Glam trappings in order to perform mindless, menial tasks such as modeling.

Disposition:

As noted above, Glam Rockers are an affable species. Despite exhibiting a generally upbeat demeanor, many specimens have been known to swing between two entirely dissimilar emotional states, sulky and hyper, with little middle ground. Glam Rockers are at all times dramatic, and it is this penchant for the theatrical which many experts blame for the species' lack of mental stasis. Dissenting opinion holds, however, that recreational drug use may be responsible for much of the Glam Rocker's pendulous instability.

Glam Rockers can be quite flaky. Best intentions aside, they are difficult to pin down and are not the type of Hipsters one should expect to show up at a specific event at a particular time. *Do not include them in your wedding party.*

Habitat:

In Los Angeles, CA:

KEY CLUB ["CHERRY"] *(9039 West Sunset Boulevard)*—On the western fringe of the strip, this veritable "starship" of a nightclub hosts LA's most "dramatic" and "decadent" glam party, where "beautiful" "boys and girls" wallow in "glorious excess," ponder their own "sexual ambiguity," and play "pop star." Regulars bemoan the crude taunts of tourists in attendance ("poofs," "pansies"), which often bruise the "sensitive," "soft" natures of local "aesthetes."

DRAGONFLY ["PRETTY UGLY CLUB"] *(6510 Santa Monica Boulevard)*—Wednesday nights bring out the "colorful," "gorgeous" people to this "grand" weekly party that is "pure ecstasy." "Elegant" boys "draped in garland" leave little to the "imagination," so take home one of these "darlings" before they "fade away." Locals claim "everyone's a superstar," even those "grungy outcasts" huddled by the bar.

In New York, NY:

DON HILL'S *(511 Greenwich Street)*—Beyond the dreary brick wall "façade" lurk "glittering frock-clad boys" in "eyeliner" and "sparkling makeup." Break out your "platform shoes" and "bisexual" curiosity; the party here is as "sumptuous" as the cover charge is "outrageous." While "tarted-up" "dandies" are the honored guests, "self-conscious" "wall-flowers" may forgo "space-age rock personas" in favor of "excessive" alcohol intake.

GOTHS

DEPRESSIVA THEATRICO

BLACK

TORTURED

BLACK

BLACK

UNFLATTERING
HORIZONTAL
STRIPES

GOTHS

Male
EXTERIOR: Goth-Industrial motif—black T-shirt; black loose-fitting cargo pants; trench coat.
ACCESSORIES: Chunky belt hung with keys; black lace-up Dr. Martens boots.
MARKINGS: Eyeliner.
PLUMAGE: Black, long, and stringy.

Female
EXTERIOR: Pale complexion, S & M gear (bustier; garter belt); PVC; tall, laced boots; fishnet or striped stockings; flowy, loose-fitting, lacy garb
MARKINGS: Heavy black eyeliner; red lipstick.
PLUMAGE: Long and black; either braided or straight; possible red streaks.

Both Sexes
VOICE: Plaintive wailing delivered via "online journal" (both sexes).

L ike many Hipsters, this species propagates itself through an intense period of adolescent unpopularity. Goths adhere to strict artistic ideals and, unlike similarly rebellious yet angrier species [*see* Punk Rockers], exhibit a rich, lush aesthetic. Despite glaring levels of social inadequacy, the species is among the most visually outrageous of our Hipsters. *They are incredibly easy to spot in the field and thus ideal for beginners.*

These Hipsters, no doubt due to repeated high school ribbing, possess particularly tortured souls. They convey the utter darkness of their station through a metaphorical and largely black wardrobe, consisting of such elements as platform boots, capes, cloaks, rubber, fishnets, corsets, and leggings. Despite the intended bleak seriousness of their markings, the species' inherent geekery often remains painfully apparent.

Creatures of the night, both symbolically and in fact, Goths affect a studied, vampirish appearance and enjoy sleeping all day. The species' preference for all things nocturnal and dark extends to the seasonal: Goths do not enjoy the warm summer months or sunlight in general. With summer comes serious clothing dilemmas, such as the sweat-streaked face makeup and frowned-upon pairing of black boots with shorts [Figure 1].

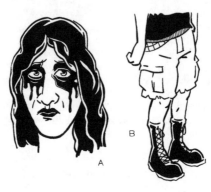

FIGURE 1

By Day:
Fishnet leggings cost money. Fortunately, years spent pursuing extremely geeky endeavors [e.g., "Dungeons and Dragons"] have conditioned the species to perform, almost instinctually, the duties of Computer Programmer or Graphic Designer. Aside from the afore-mentioned fiduciary advantages, such careers allow Goths to retain much of their preferred aesthetic, as only rarely is business casual wear required. Male specimens enjoy this luxury with greater ease than do their usually more ostentatious female counterparts; black T-shirt and black jeans, while unorthodox, may pass for office wear more read-ily than S & M gear, which most discerning supervisors frown upon.

Adaptability; Ruggedness:
Goths are considered the cockroaches of the Hipster Kingdom. Not only can they withstand periods of radical hip redefinition [e.g.,

1992–95], but they remain virtually unchanged throughout. In the wake of particularly unsavory species-specific interludes [e.g., Columbine; the mainstream pop appeal of Marilyn Manson], Goths have been known to scurry under the proverbial cupboard for cover until the worst has blown over. It has been postulated that Goths will be the only Hipsters able to survive a nuclear holocaust.

Credibility:
The species harbors a good deal of resentment over the recent mainstream popularity of what they consider "fake" Goths. Many believe that to look Goth does not necessarily equal being Goth. One must identify with the music [a cloying mix of Rimbaud-esque themes, industrial synth and sweat, the genre includes gothic rock, ethereal, dreampop, darkwave, dark synthpop, neo-classical, goth-industrial, and goth-metal], not just with the look. Participation in the actual Goth social scene is emblematic of real Goths [*see* below]; little kids dressing weird and rebelling for rebellion's sake are not. Goths do not bum rides from their parents or observe curfews.

In order to attain Gothic credibility, specimens are required to involve themselves in a regular cycle of club going, complemented by liberal postings to Goth newsgroups and ingratiation into the local social hierarchy. Serious adherents are also urged to participate in a strange practice known as "performance." Occurring in club terrain, these performances consist mainly of ritualized, interpretative, theatrical dance-like movements set to spooky music. They are undertaken in all seriousness and are carefully rehearsed.

Party Animals:
Though flamboyant, Goths can be painfully dull; death, despair, and loneliness are both conversationally stifling and quite exhausting. Even in comfortable terrain (dank basements, computer labs, etc.), the species is rarely gregarious. Many have even been observed, at parties, in the supine position upon a sofa [Figure 2].

FIGURE 2

Despite their utter lack of *joie de vivre*, Goths are fond of engaging in a series of movements which technically constitute the act of dancing. A completely joyless enterprise, their "dance" features dramatic hand motions and is only performed solo. Concerned more with methodology than fun, this lumbering display requires vast personal space and is best described as a period of controlled flailing. Though specifics vary, the "dance" usually features exaggerated arm swinging, general swishing about, affected gestures, and a great deal of crouching.

Habitat:

Due to their theatrical appearance, Goths are generally unable to blend comfortably into normal terrain and thus are forced to congregate at Goth Theme Nights. Though often held in somewhat gritty locales, this terrain is quite harmless (and dreadful). These events are given unimaginatively Gothy names [*see* below] with little hint of irony, as the species is anything but subtle. *In such terrain, dressing Goth is not only encouraged, but often required. Though white face makeup may prove a bit much, the shedding of labels such as "Banana Republic," "Gap," or "J Crew" is strongly recommended.*

In Boston, MA:

MANRAY ["CRYPT"] *(21 Brookline Street, Central Square, Cambridge)*—
Open until the "vampirish" hour of 2:00 A.M., this all-purpose countercultural complex features several "cool, damp, dark" rooms, each
perfectly suited for either "moping" or "celebrating the darkness of the
human psyche." Though "absinthe" remains "sadly" unavailable, an ice-
cold Sam Adams nicely complements any "angst-filled dissection of
Lovecraft." A "convenient cape check booth" allows patrons more freedom to express the "beauty of enduring pain" while performing the
"gothic slide" on the dance floor.

T.T. THE BEAR'S PLACE ["REVERIE"] *(10 Brookline Street, Cambridge)*—
Save the "poetry recital" for another time and check your "sadness" at
the door, as this venue boasts a sound system loud enough to be "almost life-affirming." "Blessed Goddess!" this place "really rocks." In true
Boston nightlife tradition, doors close promptly at 1:00 A.M., so stock
up on "clove cigarettes" and schedule a "late-night Wicca ceremony" for
after.

In New York, NY:

CB'S 313 GALLERY ["ALCHEMY"] *(313 Bowery)*—Ignore those "dirty,
unimaginative Punks next door" and "revel" in this Monday night event
that's "sexier than a graveyard photo." An abundance of "morbidly fascinating yet coy" types leave many patrons wondering "What would the
Marquis de Sade do?" Most choose to simply "enjoy the music" and
"contemplate pre-Raphaelite depictions of death and religion."

DOWNTIME ["ALBION/BATCAVE"] *(251 West 30th Street)*—The premier
New York "goth-industrial" showcase, this Saturday night event is
"steeped in acerbity" and "just loaded with hot chicks in fetish gear."
The line for the bathroom can be "more excruciating than a Marilyn
Manson concert," so "don't drink too much blood before arriving." "I
can't wait to post the pics in my online journal tomorrow."

METAL HEADS

HEADBANGRIA LONELYUM

THE BLACK METAL HEAD:
AVOID AT ALL COSTS

BANGING HEAD

ALL CLOTHING
IN SOME WAY
TORN

BLACK
CONCERT
T-SHIRT

FIGURE 2

METAL HEADS

EXTERIOR: Straight-legged semitight denim jeans (light blue or black); high-top sneakers; black T-shirt with distorted, devilish typeface, death imagery, skull and bones; concert T-shirt; trench coat.
PLUMAGE: Long (bangs, hair spray, perhaps "feathered").
VOICE: Short barking notes of aggressive volume.

Though sometimes confused with generic Dirtbags and Burnouts, Metal Heads exhibit surprisingly enlightened, musically obsessed qualities while retaining a decidedly loutish charm.* Despite an often garishly intimidating appearance, this species is actually quite easily approached (with the noted exception of those into "black metal" [*see* below]). *Use of the term "Rock and roll!" is recommended as an introduction. Accompanying hand gestures are optional* [Figure 1]. These Hipsters enjoy spirited, musically themed debate, sprinkled liberally with immature sexual boasting and alcohol-laced profanity.

The species is overwhelmingly male. Females typically function as

FIGURE 1

*True Metal Heads can distinguish among bands just by the crowd noise audible on a CD recording.

little more than groupies or ornamentation and, while full-fledged distaff Metal Heads do exist, most are regarded as lesbians by their male counterparts. Metal is something that certain types of men pursue in order to fill the voids in their lives. The species is comprised, primarily, of males who have found themselves unable to get along with anybody else. These Hipsters are thoroughly aware of the degenerative qualities of their passion; certain specimens, on their deathbeds, have been known to quietly ponder, "Why metal?"

The species is still reeling from the popularity enjoyed by hair metal during the 1980s [e.g., Poison, Cinderella, Whitesnake, White Lion, et al.] and resultant confusion between such acts and serious metal preferred by the true fan [e.g., Metallica, Megadeth, Slayer, Anthrax, Pantera, Sepultera, et al.].

Mating Habits:
While metal musicians enjoy copulation by the hot-tubful [e.g., Gene Simmons], the mating habits of casual Metal Heads have thus far eluded identification, though the continued propagation of the species would suggest that certain Metal Heads do indeed copulate.

Despite such passionate male on male interplay as "Metal Nights" (anxiously awaited functions at which these Hipsters congregate to drink whiskey, smoke cigarettes, and listen to and debate a preconceived program of Heavy Metal), these Hipsters do not exhibit the homoeroticism typical of similarly male-dominated species [see Ex-Frats]. Homosexuality is frowned upon as a lack of masculine prowess, though apparently a lack of female contact is de rigueur.

Breeds:
The most noteworthy of present-day breeds are Death Metal Heads and Black Metal Heads* (the species is not noted for the breadth of its inspi-

---

*Thrash (or Speed) Metal bridged the gap between founding fathers Led Zeppelin and Black Sabbath and today's two prevalent breeds. Basically a hyped-up, supercharged, yet technically traditional version of old-school metal, Thrash Metal found popularity with bands such as Metallica, Megadeth, Slayer, Pantera, Anthrax, Sepultera, etc. Fans of Thrash Metal are the typical Metal Heads regularly observed serving high school detention.

ration). The two herds are quite antagonistic; BMHs, in particular, despise their counterparts' penchant for sweat pants and sunny locales [e.g., Florida]. Black Metal Heads are far and away the most dangerous Hipsters one may encounter in the field. *Do not approach under any circumstances.* These Hipsters count murder and church arson among their favorite pastimes and should not be trifled with. Fortunately, most specimens are indigenous to Sweden, Norway, or other similarly frigid and distant terrain. Like Satanism, black metal boasts a specific, if tiresome, narrative. Black Metal Heads are white supremacist, pagan, and ultra-nationalistic; as such, their conversational repertoire leaves something to be desired. They can be extremely theatrical, often donning white "corpsepaint" and flamboyantly sinister outfits [Figure 2] [e.g., Emperor, Bathory, Burzum, etc.].

Death Metal is noteworthy more for the technical aspects of its construction than for the lackluster showmanship of its practitioners. The music features a double bass drum (two kick pedals) and inverts the traditional metal aesthetic by placing the vocals lower in range than the percussion. These Hipsters are sonically obsessed and technically astute. Their music, though far removed from metal's blues roots, retains specific metal themes and attitude [e.g., Vader, Suffocation, Morbid Angel, etc.].

Habitat:

In Houston, TX:

FITZGERALD'S *(2706 White Oak Drive)*—"Rock and roll!" at this musical "shithouse" that's sadly been "taken over by alternative sissies" of late. Still, regulars insist their "eardrums are bleeding" from the "asskickin'" sound system and "killer" "ax work" of the remaining metal acts. It can get sweaty, so "leave your trench coat in the car" and, while moshing is allowed, locals say "that ain't rock 'n' roll, man."

In Pasadena, CA:

MOOSE MCGILLYCUDDY'S ["THE ROCK ROOM"] *(119 East Colorado Boulevard)*—Though normally populated with "goddamned jocks" like "those guys who kicked my ass in high school," Sunday nights at this sports bar and happy hour fave feature the musical stylings of Metal Shop, a tribute band known to "shove metal right up your ass." "Death" and "destruction" are best wallowed in over a few rounds of famous Moose's Mai Tais. "Rock on."

In Poughkeepsie, NY:

THE CHANCE *(6 Crannell Street)*—"Hello, Poughkeepsie!" Metal Heads "keep the faith" at this "cool" theater featuring "Led Zep tributes and shit." The "absolutely awesome" sound and "kick-ass" "drunk Vassar chicks" contribute to an atmosphere that "kicks major ass."

In West Springfield, VA:

JAXX NIGHTCLUB *(6355 Rolling Road)*—"Well, aaaal-rye-hite" rave falsetto-voiced fans of this converted movie theatre that's been "rockin'" for over twenty years. A favorite of both older "mulletted" fans and local "aggressive" youths, the bar is best known as being the home turf of the Roadducks, who "rock the house" on a semiregular basis. Don't forget to do a little flirting with "that killer babe Kimmie" at the bar who "rules the universe" in between acts.

RUDE BOYS (AND GIRLS)

SKANKUS PLAIDUM

SHAVED HEAD

PICKS IT UP,
PICKS IT UP,
PICKS IT UP

"SKANKING"

Named for a violent and aggressive character (1960s Jamaican gangster types), Rude Boys and Rude Girls are actually among the most pleasant, thoughtful, and amorous Hipsters one may encounter in the field. The species is unique in that, while historically spawned by social unrest and economic turmoil, present-day specimens are wholly removed from these origins in terms of time and geography. Experts speculate that the majority of these Hipsters have not, nor ever will, actually set foot upon the Caribbean terrain from whence they metaphorically sprang.

Though consumed by a dated musical form and social epoch, the species has succeeded in bringing new life to the genre through the creation of new and innovative compositions. Rudies are often highly trained (usually in jazz) and excellent musicians. Furthermore, present-day artists [e.g., the Toasters, the Slackers, Hepcat, the Scofflaws, etc.] have received the blessings of original, still-active practitioners [e.g., the Skatalites, Sly & Robbie, Horace Andy, Stranger Cole, etc.].[*]

Music Preferred:
Though ostensibly professing some spiritual, political, and philosophical belief systems, the herd would thin considerably were music (and resultant dancing) removed from the equation. Historically a mix of traditional Jamaican rhythms and early American soul, rock, and rhythm and blues, their music has taken on several different though related forms:

SKA—Originally a Jamaican version of American and British oldies, this bass- and drum-dependent music is primarily distinguished by its unique beat, called the "skank."

ROCKSTEADY—Very traditional, less funky than reggae and slower than ska. Rumored to have originated during one particularly scorching summer in Jamaica as, too hot to play dance music, artists created a relaxing, more contemplative spin-off.

REGGAE—Slightly faster than rocksteady, reggae is closely related to, and often associated with, the Rastafarian religion. As a result, the faith profoundly influenced content.

DANCEHALL—An early precursor to rap, this dance music features a DJ, called a "Toaster," talking over records being spun. Said dialogue ("toasting") is traditionally boastful and confrontational.

DUB—Generally performed by DJs, not musicians, dub features scratching, mixing, level manipulation, and heady amounts of looping and reverb.

Temperament; Natural Enemy:
Technically speaking, Rudies are a relatively "chill" species. Experts speculate that their loose, relaxed disposition may be somehow connected to their near-constant marijuana inhalation. However, sudden violent out-

[*]The species bristles at comparisons to the semirecent swing revival.

breaks have been observed and, though general approach is recommended, *the wearing of a porkpie hat is urged for safety.*

Their music (particularly reggae) is often political and vaguely revolutionary; class equality, rights for the poor, anticapitalism, and hatred of "the Man" are heavily featured. The antiracist motif, coupled with a proximity to the Punk scene, sometimes leads to confrontation with the species' one true natural enemy, the Nazi Skinhead [*see* entry]. Said confrontations are usually highbrow, articulate affairs laced with periodic boot or blade play for punctuation. *Steer clear of such entanglements.*

Habitat:

Despite their richness of heritage, Rudies are a relatively rare Hipster. While vast, free-ranging herds are rumored to exist far afield in Europe, domestic specimens are often relegated to small, reserved pockets of urban terrain.

In Boston, MA:
BILL'S BAR *(5 Lansdowne Street)*—This rock venue earns major "respect" for fostering a scene "independent" from the surrounding dance clubs. The Sunday reggae event is a "local" "tradition," providing "oppressed" college kids the "opportunity" to "rebel" by "dancing" and drinking "Pete's Wicked Ale." Regulars call for "unity" and "no class on Mondays."

In Los Angeles, CA:
SHORT STOP ["DUB CLUB"] *(1455 Sunset Boulevard)*—This "kick ass," "up-tempo" Wednesday party features all the joys of "Babylon" and no cover to boot. "Dem a drink and dance" to an "equal" mix of musical styles. Though most love the lack of doorman, some "protest" all the "skanks" allowed in. Still, next to a "Kingston" "ghetto," this place "rocks steady."

In New York, NY:
SOUTHPAW *(125 Fifth Avenue, Brooklyn)*—Located in the former "shanty-town" district of Park Slope, this bar/lounge features great live acts and is ideal for lamenting "colonial"-bred "economic domination," discussing "Rastafarianism," or falling under the "influence" of the extensive Brooklyn-brewed beer selection. The "black and tan" get together "harmoniously," note the "brotherhood" of drinkers lined up at the bar.

In San Francisco, CA:

BLAKES ON TELEGRAPH *(2367 Telegraph Avenue, Berkeley)*—For live music and Happy Hour prices "right out of the Third World," this college bar is "better than ganja." "Gwan," try a burger or the teriyaki chicken; the "international" draft selections and "offbeat" cocktails wash it down better than "Trench Town's sewage system." Local "hepcats" appreciate the social "freedom" afforded by the regular 2:00 A.M. closing time.

THUGZ

DRIVEBYLUM HOODICUS

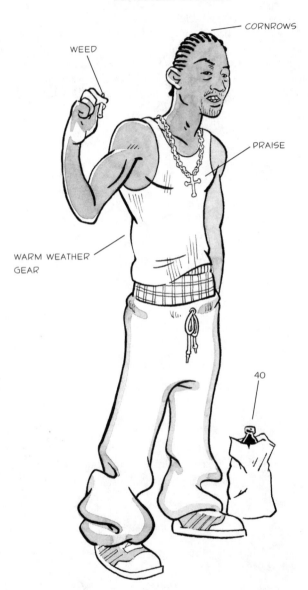

CORNROWS

WEED

PRAISE

WARM WEATHER GEAR

40

An often vile and petulant species, Thugz provide source material for the violent "gangsta" posturings of certain hard-core rap artists [e.g., Death Row Records, NWA, Eazy-E, Jay-Z, Ice-T, etc.]. These arbiters of urban cool inspire, at once, both youthful zest and suburban parental concern [e.g., Joseph and Linda Aiello, ca. 1987]. Though certain aspects of their lifestyle have been glossed over into pop-friendly form [e.g., The Gourds' twangy cover of Snoop Dogg's "Gin and Juice," the gangbanger posturings of *Office Space* and *Boiler Room*, Will Smith, etc.], observers should remain aware that these Hipsters are the genuine article and *may be dangerous to approach.* Many, especially West Coast specimens, are actual gang members and extremely territorial [*see* A. Mutterperl's landmark study *The Cap in My Ass*].

Female specimens do exist, but are kept strictly lower level, employed mainly as decoys or drug transports.

Some specimens suffer from a little understood oral irregularity which causes chronic mispronunciation of certain sounds [e.g., *a* instead of *er* or *z* instead of *s*].

Interests:
Thugz exhibit an affinity for the outdoors and enjoy smoking blunts, copulating with females [termed "bitches"], and blasting rap music from either car stereos (finances permitting) or portable disc players.

Of further interest is the species' impressive ability to simultaneously play Celo while consuming alcoholic malt beverages from forty-ounce containers swathed in brown-paper wrappers.

Though certainly intimidating, Thugz do not represent the most extreme element of the hip-hop underworld [a distinction usually reserved to Project Cats, a non-Hip and highly dangerous species]. Many of these Hipsters do mingle with more mainstream types and celebrities, often to the point of forming a symbiotic relationship [e.g., Carson Daly]. By fostering such associations, celebrities not otherwise viewed as being "down" receive copious levels of street cred (or "mad props"), while Thugz are granted a larger audience to which they may boast of living dangerously.

Habitat:

In Ione, CA:
MULE CREEK STATE PRISON *(4001 State Highway 104)*—This "West Coast" "pen," where "Bloods" do "2 to 4" after "gettin' caught with a bird in the hand" by "the po-po" is "all that." Whether "sippin' on some pruno" in your "country blues" or getting "cock diesel" in the gym, regulars say "GTA" "was the case that they gave me," "chulo." After "dropping science, but not soap" in the shower, some locals claim "I'm a get busy" in the literacy program.

In New York, NY:
STREET CORNER *(125th Street and St. Nicholas Avenue)*—"Gs up, Hos down" at this "chill" location where "niggaz" "be gatherin'" to "smoke Indo" and "load their 12-gauges." Regulars "give props" to "The Boogie Down" before hopping into a "ghetto sled" and taking off with "that girl from 'round the way," though most "homeys" prefer just "gettin' loc-ed" while "cold lampin'."

The *Auteurial* Family

FIVE SPECIES:

1. DJS (HIPSTER/SOCIALITE)

2. LAPTOP ROCK ARTISTS

3. LITERATI

4. STARVING ARTISTS

5. STRUGGLING ACTORS (FILM AND STAGE)

ALSO DISCUSSED:

1. DJS (HIP-HOP/BATTLE)

2. STRUGGLING ACTORS (MUSICAL THEATRE)

This family is noted for its intense impulse to create. Expressed through various artistic means, the work produced by these Hipsters is often of a sophomoric variety. However, certain specimens do manage to surprise and, as a result, the species' efforts are generally encouraged. Inclusion in this family does not necessarily connote actual artistic output, but merely a professed and fastidious desire to someday do so. [Note: certain experts place Corporate Hipsters in this family. While not strictly forbidden, the classification is considered somewhat unorthodox.]

DJs (HIPSTER/SOCIALITE)

OMNIPRESENTUM FASHIONABLUS

ENCYCLOPEDIC
KNOWLEDGE OF
RARE RECORDINGS

SUITABLY
OBSCURE
RECORD

VINYL

EXTERIOR: Good sneakers; casual dress.
PLUMAGE: Scraggly and shaggy.
ACCESSORIES: Record-filled milk crate; DJ satchel.

Noted for compulsively wallowing in the audio technology of a bygone era, this species has recently entered a period of intense propagation; once something of a cultural curiosity, these Hipsters are now socially ubiquitous. They have completely saturated the club/bar scene and can even be spotted in such unusual terrain as Urban Outfitters and Diesel Style Lab. Like a cocktail napkin, every function needs one.

DJs are among the most elitist of our Hipsters. Public dissemination, termed "spinning," affords them the opportunity to impress upon the masses their particular and ultra-specific obsessions [e.g., Speed Garage, Two Step, etc.]. Records, or "vinyl," represent the species' preferred vehicle of audio playback. Certain DJs do spin CDs, but such cretins are generally scoffed at.*

Pecking Order:
This strain of the species is noted more for sublime taste than technical wizardry. Though capable of light mixing, these are primarily not the DJs who sell records of their creations. (CDs sold by these Hipsters amount to little more than slickly produced mixed tapes and therefore *purchase is not recommended*.) As such, these Hipsters are sometimes disparaged by their alpha cousins, the Hip-Hop (or Battle) DJ, though this highly evolved creature tends to tolerate its less advanced (though equally trendy) relations, and violence is generally averted.

---

*DJs who play weddings or bar mitzvahs are of no real social or artistic import. Such specimens are rightly derided and despised.

Nesting:

DJs spend considerable time holed up in cramped yet creatively decorated hovels. It is in such environments that they engineer and fuss over their chosen system of record organization, often a complex and labyrinthine affair conducted over a prolonged period of hibernation. The organizational schematic is as much a part of personal pride to the Hipster as the collection itself. No self-respecting DJ arranges his records alphabetically. Instead, most prefer absurdist genre-based systems of classification [e.g., chronological arrangement according to favored genre of boys dated].

Mating Habits:

DJs are often startlingly attractive and some even boast celebrity lineage [e.g., Paul Sevigny, Cameron Douglas, Mark Ronson, et al.]. Specimens not blessed with godlike urban cuteness make up for their physical shortcomings with enviable style, and as a result the scene is quite fashionable on the whole. While traditionally male, female DJs not only exist but are, at present, quite trendy. They are often unbelievably adorable and occasionally Asian to boot. *Repeated observation may prove unavoidable.*

Technique:

Professional DJs bring their own needles to gigs. These expensive and fragile instruments are installed pre-set during an ostentatious flurry of arrangement in the DJ booth, as the Hipster methodically arranges his records (in milk crates or fancy padded cases), checks the sound, adjusts the headphones (also brought from home), and acts in a generally cool manner.

Though the set is often predetermined, DJs take great pains to give off an air of ad hoc creativity. In the past, these Hipsters were quite secretive, often applying label-obscuring tape to their records. Today, however, onlookers are free to inquire as to what is being played with impunity. *Never request a song unless engaging in the process of sexual flirtation. Pay close attention to genre; do not request Motley Crue if the DJ is spinning Soul.*

Habitat:

DJs are best observed while at work. When not so obviously appointed, these Hipsters may prove largely indistinguishable from several other species [*see* AlternaBoys, Indie Rockers, et al.].

In Chicago, IL:

GET ME HIGH LOUNGE *(1758 North Honore)*—This converted three-story "house" features an eclectic "mix" of music and an "intimate," "after-party" atmosphere ideal for "scratching" other plans to "kick it" in comfort here. Most sets are "definitely better than that breakup tape I made in junior high," and the "sumptuous" cocktails have been known to lull some patrons into a "trance."

In Los Angeles, CA:

LIQUID KITTY *(11780 West Pico Boulevard)*—For a "chill" night of low-key boozing, this pitch-black martini bar is "the shit." With R & B or Soul "wax" on "the platter," weeknights are perfect for slowing down the "tempo" and ruminating upon the finer points of "beatmatching." Some recommend "sleeping with the DJ" in exchange for "drink tickets."

In New York, NY:

13 ["SHOUT!"] *(35 East 13th Street)*—This free Sunday night 1960s Soul party is regarded as "the bomb" by fans of "fresh" music and Downtowners who consider the club's usual $10 cover "too corporate." Though the genre is derided by some as "more passé than a belt-driven turntable," the "seamless" sets insure a "vibe" greatly suited to dancing with "sweet" women.

In Philadelphia, PA:

FLUID *(613 South Fourth Street)*—So tiny "I had to leave my other crate in the car," the "sick" "decks" work on display at this unmarked bar make it one of the city's most "badass" scenes. The crowd, while often "freaky," is not nearly as "impressive as this track structure." Though conversation may sometimes be limited by "tinnitus," locals rave "look, it's Jazzy Jeff!" Rumors persist that "befriending the barkeep" may result in "free drinks."

LAPTOP ROCK ARTISTS

PRECOCIUM ROBOTO

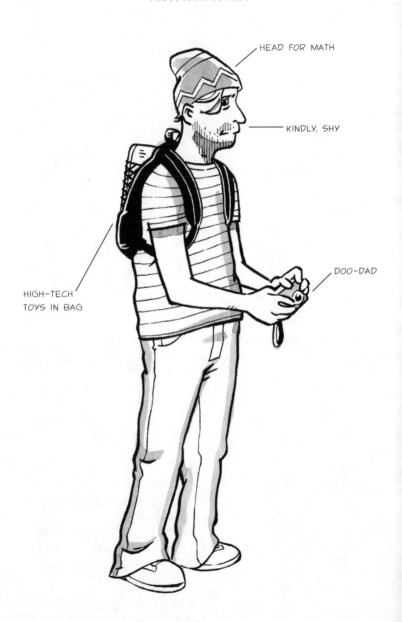

HEAD FOR MATH

KINDLY, SHY

DOO-DAD

HIGH-TECH
TOYS IN BAG

LAPTOP ROCK ARTISTS

EXTERIOR: Indistinct—colored or striped T-shirt; denim jeans.
PLUMAGE: Prematurely balding; facial hair (beard).
ACCESSORIES: Eyeglasses (all variety); wool hat; scarf (weather permitting); laptop computer in over-the-shoulder bag.
VOICE: Practically indecipherable.

The most esoteric and intellectually forbidding of all Hipsters, Laptop Rock Artists are consumed both by audio and their own intelligentsia. Though technically not cyborg, these Hipsters are connected to their computers in a perfectly symbiotic nature, as each stretches the other to its full potential. In fact, most specimens are unidentifiable when not in the company of their laptop (usually Apple PowerBooks).

Much of their conversation borders on the indecipherable. When not creating music, some enjoy studying/teaching robotics and artificial intelligence at eastern institutions of particular prestige [e.g., M.I.T.]. The species is quite conscious of its mental prowess; in fact, one subset of their electronica is humbly referred to as Intelligent Dance Music (IDM) [*see* http://music.hyperreal.org/lists/idm/]. Most Laptop Rock Artists inspire intellectual appreciation rather than physical lunacy.

Origin of the Species:
Sired by the advent of sound-editing software and appropriately high-speed processors, Laptop Rock Artists are an advanced offshoot of the more traditional DJ [*see* entry], simple creatures who have yet to abandon a thoroughly quaint and arcane level of technology [i.e., vinyl, analog recordings], and are rumored also to retain vestigial tails. These Hipsters serve a similar function as do their ancestors, merely having replaced the turntable with the laptop computer. Unlike DJs, however,

many LRAs craft their music entirely pre-performance, then play back the creation in front of a live audience.

Performance:

Use of the term "performance" is here applied loosely, since the spectacle of computer geeks sitting at a desk onstage leaves a bit to be desired. For observers holding on to the concepts of human-based communication and personal, physical interaction, the scene may prove mysterious and depressing. The occasional flourish of mouse clicking does little to alleviate the monotony.

In efforts to lend shows an element of the theatrical, many artists are accompanied by video projection.[*] Often as technically ambitious as the music itself, these videos are nonlinear and experimental in persuasion.

Lack of Mobility:

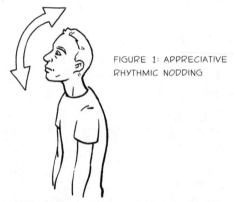

FIGURE 1: APPRECIATIVE
RHYTHMIC NODDING

The species does not engage in traditional modes of musical appreciation and, in fact, the physical act of dancing is undertaken only by neophytes, morons, or their girlfriends. Spectators here replace such

---

[*]In lieu of video, LRAs sometimes add vitality to their performances through more conventional means. Some hook up with rappers, while others, such as Chicks on Speed, actually sing. Hipsters in the audience have been known to actually enjoy themselves at such shows.

clumsy antics with a studious and rigid method of audio appreciation [Figure 1]. Typically, three to four specimens will cluster in a small group, often arranged in a semicircular arrangement. While engaged in said schematic, most specimens will assume postures featuring heavy doses of chin rubbing, eyebrow raising, laptop bag strap fingering, and nonsexual longing. Though technically open to all, these clusters are often hierarchical in nature. That is, most Hipsters tend to congregate with LRAs who approximate their own level of intelligence. These groups may be intimidating and are, indeed, quite impenetrable.

Habitat:

As practitioners of a relatively new and innovative form, Laptop Rock Artists have yet to settle on an appropriate venue in which to stage their antics. Their music does not easily lend itself to either traditional dance clubs or concert halls. Though well suited for residential terrain (especially in event of long, lonely Friday nights), public displays have thus far been largely relegated to acceptable, yet somewhat ill-fitting, rock and roll clubs.

In Dallas, TX:
TREES *(2709 Elm Street)*—Ostensibly a rock and roll club, this Deep Ellum institution lends itself quite nicely to the "digitized mnemorealms" of "badass" "electro beats" and "delightfully retarded" video "pieces," though some find the "arboreal" design "schematic" to be as "tedious" as that "dork" who "posted" a request for "WAV to MP3 encoding software suitable for Win98 platforms."

In Milwaukee, WI:
CIRCLE A *(932 East Chambers Street)*—This small neighborhood bar is so cozy it reminds some regulars of "the Little Sound DJ modification for GameBoy." The ultra-cheap drink specials and a jukebox featuring all of your "analog" favorites create an ideal environment in which to discuss the fact that "I am far less interested in audio as 'soundtrack' than I am in using the audio for purposes of creating more adaptive interfaces."

In New York, NY:

TONIC *(107 Norfolk Street)*—"Which web server hosts your distro?" ask huddled "IDMers" exploring "the intersection between sound and individual moments of spontaneous experience" at this "rad" performance space. The adjacent fringe bookstore is "top tier," even if it "lamentably" doesn't stock "*Igloo* magazine." Some adventurous "audiofiles" suggest "sampling" some alcohol during the "set," while others warn that the bathrooms aren't up to "code."

In Oakland, CA:

BLACK BOX *(1928 Telegraph Avenue)*—This community art space is the perfect venue for "chatting nostalgically about the C64," discussing "the interactive elements, or virtuality, of level design," or simply relaxing with a cup of coffee while pondering "the unfortunate fact that video game audio is boiling down to either Sound IDs for objects or simple background music" in the café. Of course, live shows are the main draw; some rave that the "meso-narrative" videos are "miniexcursions into real-time dream-state."

LITERATI

AUTHOREAUX PARASITUM

HEAD-SCRATCHING IMPLEMENT

JOURNAL

"SOUL PATCH"

TWEED

BEAT "LITERATURE"

a novel by
P. J. O'Grady
Patrick J. O'Grady
P. Joseph O'Grady
Joey
rick Joseph O'

O f all extinct species, none was as deserving of its demise as the contemptible and repugnant Beatniks [*Literatum posturo*]. Given that the Literati is instinctually drawn to the Beat culture (some have even been observed in possession of a Jack Kerouac coffee mug), the species is not particularly recommended for observation.* In fact, the very classification of these creatures as Hip is a source of great dispute among prominent hipthologists [e.g., James Marchese's seminal *Even Worse Than Transcendentalism*]. However, the species' migration to, and complete immersion in, otherwise hip, caffeine-drenched terrain [*see* Habitat] makes exclusion unrealistic.

Plumage; Coat:

The Literati is noted for presenting an overall tweedy appearance, and the species remains quite ignorant of the universal disgust directed at suede elbow patches. Likewise, their staunch insistence on donning sports jackets regardless of environment remains a constant source of derision. Exceptionally aloof specimens will occasionally go so far as to pair said article with denim blue jeans. *Such habits are not to be emulated.*

In further attempts to appear professorial, Literati exhibit eyewear regardless of necessity. Frames are either of the dark plastic or anachro-

*It is important to note that the species' attempts to emulate the Beat lifestyle generally do not include homosexuality or actually having work published.

nistically wire-rimmed variety. When striving to impart an impression of their own tortured intelligence, the species will remove their glasses in order to facilitate wearied brow rubbing. Also, when ostensibly riveted by some hardbound text, certain specimens will commence in the sliding of eyewear nostril-ward before proceeding to squint over the frames. Both actions are preceded by furtive glances designed to ascertain the curiosity of those located in the immediate proximity.

In keeping with their desire to appear somewhat reluctantly bookish, these Hipsters are also noted for a constantly shifting repertoire of head and facial hair [Figure 1]. While precise examples vary, the look is consistently scruffy and meant to imply a theoretically dangerous countenance. *They are, however, quite harmless and generally not of fighting shape.* This continual whisker molting does little to obscure their appearance or hinder identification.

FIGURE 1

Raison d'être:

These Hipsters are legends in their own hard drives. The species professes a profound interest in the concept of publication, though in practice the event is largely avoided, excepting occasional forays into little-read and highly esoteric, even homemade, anthologies [e.g., *Reflections and Lament*; *The 229 East Tenth Street Apt. 6B Review*; *Rinky Dink*; *Prior Dreams Recanted*; *Impressive, Isn't It?*; *Typings, 1999*; *From Steve's Zip Drive*, et al.]. Most specimens rationalize this disparity through invocation of the future. They will, entreaty or no, expound upon their not-too-distant and looming success. Interestingly, the precise point of arrival of this highly anticipated moment remains fixed, independent of age. That is, as the Hipster grows old, its distance from success remains constant.

Chirping:

Literati are among the most vocal of all Hipsters.* They possess extremely durable vocal chords and are able to ruminate boastfully without threat of physical repercussion. In fact, the "sore throat" is not within the species' rather large repertoire of ailments [e.g., caffeine shakes, bloodshot eyes, mental fatigue, sore writing hand, crippling ennui, et al.].

Migration:

Literati are obsessed with the concept of traveling abroad, preferably to Europe or some other terrain featuring a high café concentration. They exist in a constant cycle of trip planning and return. All stages of this cycle, with the exception of the trip itself, are complemented by long-winded ruminations on either the intricacies of their itinerary or the bittersweet sentimentality of their departure. Many excursions are undertaken in order to jump-start the creative process. Apparently, far-flung locales provide these Hipsters with inspiration unavailable domestically [i.e., girls/boys with accents].

Habitat:

Literati are lonely and secluded Hipsters. As mentioned above, cafés are a particularly rife environment for observation. Coffee is a relatively inexpensive diversion, and a largely lax turnover policy assures the species ample time for loitering. Most are unable to relax before first blanketing their table with several notepads (closed), a pen, and whichever book they are currently carrying [e.g., *Infinite Jest*, *House of Leaves*, *A Heartbreaking Work of Staggering Genius*, *Everything Is Illuminated: A Novel*, *A Confederacy of Dunces*, etc.]. Though some mindless scribbling is likely to occur, the notebooks function primarily for show. This goes for the book as well; Literati enjoy being viewed in the act of reading more than they do reading itself.

---

*When relegated to the role of "listener," Literati grow antsy and impatient. Prior to abrupt departure, most specimens will exhibit increasingly poor posture, pronounced exhalation, and furious lens cleaning.

In Chicago, IL:

QUIMBY'S BOOKSTORE *(1854 West North Avenue)*—"I hope he'll sign it 'Dear Colleague,'" confide "jittery" "bookish" types waiting in line at one of this "timeworn" shop's "eclectic" author events, which some patrons feel are "practically social." The inclusion of "esoteric" "titles" provides "validation" for certain locals' "own fears of genius-fueled alienation," while the extensive selection of "Japanese manga" has been known to "fog my eyeglasses."

In Lowell, MA:

EDSON CEMETERY [JACK KEROUAC'S GRAVE] *(Gorman Street)*—"I'm going to frame this pencil impression" and "hang it above my micro-fridge," note visitors to this final resting place/English-major pilgrimage hotspot. Though often "dark and dreary," the locale has been known to provide "inspiration" for many a "stream of consciousness narrative." The outdoor, "minimally bleak" setting is ideal for "solitary reflection," "copious note-taking," or "sophomoric hero worship."

In New York, NY:

HOUSING WORKS USED BOOKS CAFÉ *(126 Crosby Street)*—Pick an "old favorite" like *"Ham on Rye"* off the shelf, grab a "coffee, black," and settle into "an easy chair" to savor the fact that "David Chase is reading my screenplay." The small, tucked-away tables are perfect for "meeting my ex-girlfriend in hopes of a reconciliation," while a stroll through the used record aisle "affords an illusion of well-roundedness." Don't forget to "lean intelligently" against the bookshelves while "fantasizing about literary agents."

KGB BAR *(85 East Fourth Street)*—This former headquarters of the Ukrainian Working Men's Club now hosts the city's best reading series and the "sophisticates" who "sort of listen" while "outlining" their "novels." The red walls are "a perfect metaphor for my central character's descent into madness," while the draft beer provides a "better cure for writer's block" than "marijuana and an audio recording of *Howl*."

STARVING ARTISTS

NARCISSUSTUM MASTURBATIA

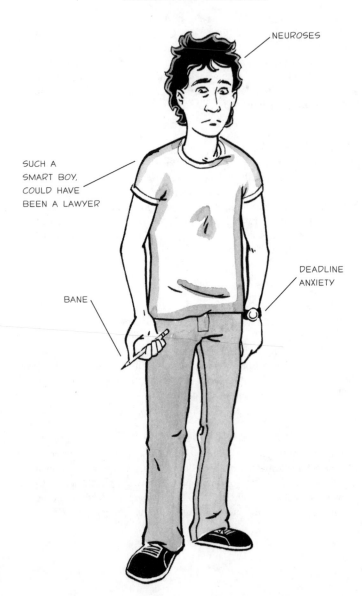

NEUROSES

SUCH A
SMART BOY,
COULD HAVE
BEEN A LAWYER

DEADLINE
ANXIETY

BANE

tarving Artists are difficult to classify according to physical specifics, as they are defined more by mission than style. Their inability to accessorize, coupled with an innate lack of money, makes their presence something of a rarity in most social environments. The species may be easily mistaken for other Hipsters [*see* Literati, Struggling Actors, Indie Rockers], and it may therefore become necessary to make actual contact with suspected specimens. *Some are surprisingly meek; approach slowly as to not frighten them.*

Population:

Modern specimens spend twice as much time sitting around coffee shops discussing their "work" than they do actually producing any. While certain Hipsters still paint and sculpt, the paradigm today has shifted toward the more pop-friendly pursuits of writing (usually screenplays, essays, or reliably dreadful poetry) and filmmaking.

The lack of cohesion inherent to this species may make observation at times seem practically impossible. As a rule of thumb, Starving Artists break down into two types:

1. Those who suffer for their art as a point of pride.

2. Those who happen to currently suffer for their art, but would really prefer to keep said suffering to a minimum.

FIGURE 1: IN THIS EXPERIMENT, AN ENDOMORPHIC SPECIMEN
OPTS FOR A FILET-O-FISH OVER HIS MANUSCRIPT, WHICH NEEDS
REVISING.

"The Law of Diminishing Abs" states that a Starving Artist's flab
mass fluctuates in a manner disproportionate to his artistic seriousness
[Figure 1]. Owing to what sociologists refer to as the "Ramen Constant," Type 2 Starving Artists appear less physically appealing than
their Type 1 counterparts. While possessing, at least in theory, a genuine desire to create good work, Type 2s struggle with the very concept
of struggling. This subgroup craves pop success outright, if only in order to fund their insatiable desire for cheeseburgers deluxe.

Raison d'être:
Despite protestations to the contrary, many Starving Artists are driven
more by a manic desire to exact revenge on the villains of their youth
than by any enlightened artistic calling. Even the most idealistic Starving Artists at times fantasize mailing favorable reviews to ex-girlfriends.
A very fine line separates Starving Artists from Vindictive Pricks. Either
way, as with the Literati [*see* entry], Starving Artists invoke the future
with a fervor normally reserved for Seventh-Day Adventists. Around
each corner lurks artistically financed independence, while obscured

behind every gloomy cloud lingers the fantasy of stunningly attractive and envy-inducing dates to future high school reunions.

Oftentimes, these Hipsters congregate to exchange ideas, lament the current state of art, reject consumerism, or devise intricate schedules for the output of future work before retiring to their couches to watch television [e.g., *Blind Date*, *MTV Cribs*, *Late Night with Conan O'Brien*, *The Daily Show with Jon Stewart*, *Curb Your Enthusiasm*, etc.].

Defense Mechanism; Natural Enemy:
When surrounded by their own kind, Starving Artists engage in a level of whining not normally observed outside the pages of children's literature [e.g., *The Princess and the Pea*]. However, the species has developed a rather elegant behavioral response to fend off more successful predators. At the first hint of implied inadequacy, Starving Artists launch into a timeworn, passive-aggressive treatise, in which they rationalize their current state of affairs in painstaking, sobering detail. Normally, said treatise will include an itemized account of just how, exactly, a well-paying and respectable corporate job sucks the soul out of life while temporary, menial, low-paying, and anxiety-inducing employment serves not only to foster the creative spirit but also to separate oneself culturally from one's fellow teeming masses. This is especially effective against their truest natural enemy, the Corporate Hipster [*see* entry].

Complex Attitude Toward Hipness:
That Starving Artists lack any palpable sense of style does not necessarily indicate any preconceived anti-trend stance. Though they may indeed mock fashion as unnecessarily obvious and question the logic of certain species' adherence to a strict uniform [*see* Punk Rockers, Outlaw Bikers], these Hipsters often harbor secret ambitions to express themselves through dress. However, they remain too acutely self-aware and fashion-deprived to act out on such impulses. Thus the ever-present solid colored T-shirt, with or without pocket. Also blue jeans; cords; earth tones.

Mating Habits:

Starving Artists will not hesitate to play up the romantic aspects of their circumstances. While most observers, as well as these Hipsters themselves, realize that most specimens are not, in fact, regularly slumped over some dimly lit desk, in jeans and tattered T-shirt, subsisting on little more than caffeine and speed, and sacrificing creature comforts for art, the fact remains that many cute young urbanites find this caricature, for whatever reason, highly attractive. Thus, many of the species' sexual liaisons result from a premeditated and ephemeral putting on of these traits [e.g., paint-splashed jeans, ink-stained fingertips, rejected credit cards, et al.]. During their intricate mating dance, little mention is made of days spent temping.

Habitat:

Starving Artists are drawn to the artistic cachet of Henry Miller-esque urban suffering [i.e., subleased apartments, liquid meals, handouts, the occasional extramarital affair]. Usually hailing from middle-class, suburban backgrounds, the species flocks to the centers of commerce, industry, and bohemia much like the immigrants to America, though without the work ethic.

In Los Angeles, CA:
INSOMNIA CAFÉ *(7286 Beverly Boulevard)*—"Let's get together and do some brainstorming" at this "home away from home" for writers with "a really great idea for a script" involving "get this: a heist gone totally wrong, plus a certain amount of bumbling and also perhaps a kidnapping." Though "I can't really afford it anyway," most regulars feel that the food "isn't really the attraction" and recommend just "getting a small coffee and sipping it very, very slowly" while attempting to "re-address my third act by introducing a twin separated at birth."

In New York, NY:

THE LIBRARY *(7 Avenue A)*—"What did you say?" ask patrons at this loud, dark East Village homage to literacy, B movies, and sexual frustration. The bartender is "so sexy I lost track of my ennui" and "tipped her Vegas-style." Noted for its "awesome" jukebox and "flattering lack of light," the bar is "just like film school, but with alcohol and girls."

LOTUS CAFÉ *(35 Clinton Street)*—This Lower East Side café/bar offers "cheap, good coffee," "plenty of places to plug in your laptop," and an "artistic by association," literate ambience. Though "I casually placed my book proposal on the bar," the "preposterously cute" bartender seemed "somehow unimpressed." "If I come back at the same time every day for the next month, she's sure to realize how cool I am."

LUNA LOUNGE ["EATING IT"] *(171 Ludlow Street)*—Monday nights at Luna Lounge feature a gathering of NY's best underground comics and the Starving Artists who stand near them. Feel free to rap with Todd Barry after the show, "well, maybe not tonight, but I'll definitely approach him next week." The $7 cover includes a free drink, or two if you "bring your diabetic friend." The alcohol helps keep "depression" in check after realizing how "less talented than Demetri Martin" you are.

STRUGGLING ACTORS
(FILM AND STAGE)

THESPIUM METHODUX

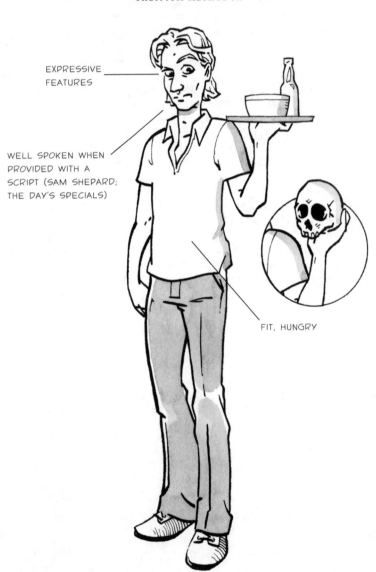

EXPRESSIVE FEATURES

WELL SPOKEN WHEN PROVIDED WITH A SCRIPT (SAM SHEPARD; THE DAY'S SPECIALS)

FIT, HUNGRY

ike most artistic types, these Hipsters migrate to urban centers upon high school graduation. This species usually follows one of two main routes, in the direction of either Los Angeles or New York City [*see* below], though certain specimens will deviate from this norm, opting instead for such locales as Chicago.

While in the throes of a process termed "auditioning" by experts, these Hipsters face rejection with a frequency usually reserved for Caucasian basketball players. While recognizing this denial as part and parcel of their chosen station, many SAs find themselves in a near-constant state of frantic self-analysis. They are among our most emotional Hipsters and are often irrationally oversensitive (a characteristic they refer to as being "passionate").

Raison d'être:
Landing a leading role in a feature film is the species' prime directive. Thus, for all their highbrow posturing, even NY specimens will sell out at the slightest hint of big-time LA money. If successful, the Hipster then proceeds to return periodically to NY, possibly to do a bit of theatrical slumming or to make the talk show rounds. Regardless of subsequent time spent in California, the specimen will continue to refer to

itself as a "New Yorker" and will perhaps maintain an apartment in the city as evidence.

Mating Habits:
As a generally attractive species, Struggling Actors enjoy sexual conquests unknown to most Hipsters [*see* Internet Geeks, Metal Heads]. Of particular import is the ritualized dance performed upon the casting couch [Figure 1]. It is on this commonplace apparatus that many spec-

FIGURE 1

imens, particularly females, trade sexual favors for career advancement.* The casting couch itself usually belongs to any number of symbiotic species, though it is most commonly employed by Casting Directors, Producers, Talent Agents, or Directors. Though typical, the particulars of casting couch liaisons are kept largely confidential, due to the small, incestuous nature of the industry. Discretion is of utmost importance.

*The term "casting couch" is metaphoric; such activity may occur on chairs, desks, tables, stages, in closets, under desks, on airplanes, in bathrooms, or the backseats of pricey sedans.

Herd Mentality:

The herd fluctuates emotionally between brotherhood and competition. This dynamic is usually predicated on success; while struggling, these Hipsters are an extremely close-knit and supportive group. They read lines together, share contacts, provide general encouragement and shoulders to cry on, rationalize facial imperfections or regional twangs, etc. However, with even the slightest hint of success comes newfound resentment from one's peers. This holds true for both intimates and strangers. At open auditions, friendliness exists inversely to the seriousness (in career terms) of the roles available.

By Day:

Until the day when heartwrenching monologues or breezy light comedy qualify as legal tender, the species must pay for such trivialities as rent and food with actual money. To meet such pedestrian requirements, these Hipsters are often forced to fulfill what they refer to as "day jobs," usually in the form of waiting tables, temp work, corporate office work, or employment at an acting studio (loving, teaching environments designed to coddle and refine the species). Given their need for flexible hours, their desire for cash money, and their spotty résumés, a majority of these Hipsters choose jobs waiting tables.

Instinct:

The species has developed an unusually well-developed means of professional, moral, ethical, and social guidance. Referred to as *Back Stage*, this weekly guide provides Struggling Actors with audition listings, acting school advertisements, acting coach testimonials, and general "we're all in it together" good cheer. Aside from functioning as a sixth sense, *Back Stage* represents the most prevalent example of the species' innate desire to network. Behind the stated function of each magazine-listed event lurks a subtle undercurrent of "please come out and meet me; we'll exchange cards and head shots."

Related Hipster:
These Hipsters are closely related, in terms of mission, to Musical Theatre Struggling Actors (*Thespium Melodius*). Noted for often outrageously flamboyant natures, these Hipsters instinctually flock to New
York in order to chase their dreams on "the Great White Way," where it
is estimated that a mere 10 to 15 percent actually make it. For the less
fortunate, a lifetime of dinner theatre and Carnival Cruise shows
awaits. The species is made up primarily of women and delightfully
catty gay men, though straight males are rumored to exist.

Natural Enemy:
In their constant pursuit of employment, the species encounters one
main enemy: the Model [*see* entry]. Due to physical perfection, said in-
terlopers are often handed choice roles regardless of possessing any inherent talent. Struggling Actors rightfully view these predators as
fraudulent, though they remain powerless to prevent Models from cir-
cumventing years of struggle through adorable flirtation and an ability
to sell women's magazines. As further insult, certain Models have
proven reliable actresses, thus calling into question the validity of the
SA's disdain [*see* Cameron Diaz, Milla Jovovich, Mena Suvari, Isabella
Rossellini, Halle Berry, etc.].

Habitat:
Unlike their Musical cousins, whose ecosystem is tailored to both work
and play, these Struggling Actors are transient and, as a result, solitary
creatures. Most specimens work in terrain (referred to as "on location")
which is varied and far flung. Relationships fostered in such environments, while often intense, rarely continue postproduction.

    The following should be considered as representing, at best, an ap-
proximation of preferred environment, based largely upon anecdotal
evidence.

In Los Angeles, CA:

SCHWAB'S DRUGSTORE / VIRGIN MEGASTORE COMPLEX *(8000 West Sunset Boulevard)*—After another round of "heart-wrenching and soul-crushing rejection," this "revamped" "Hollywood" institution is the perfect place to "rediscover my motivation" by "applying for a job at Wolfgang Puck's" or "stalking Ben Affleck." Though not as "brilliant" as in days past, this entertainment complex is "like a second home. Or a first home, actually, I just got evicted."

In New York, NY:

FITZGERALD'S PUB *(336 Third Avenue)*—"James Dean would have loved this place" claim "slouched loners" "brooding" in the corner booth at this "leading" Irish pub, where the beer is "extra" cold and the waitresses are always ready for a little "action." Though centrally located, "infantile" patrons who lack "motivation" may require more "direction."

THE SCREENING ROOM *(54 Varick Street)*—Despite the fact that "I really can't afford to hang out here," special occasions, such as "this film I did last year is screening," allow "cast and crew" a night out with a "bit" of luxury. Even though "it was only a supporting role," patrons give "good reviews" to the "genius" bartender and hors d'oeuvres that "kick Craft Service's ass." Some claim "I think the Head of Distribution for Sony Classics just looked at me."

The *Bollocksium* Family

THREE SPECIES:

1. PUNK ROCKERS

2. SKINHEADS

3. STRAIGHT-EDGE

ALSO DISCUSSED:

1. CRUSTY PUNKS

2. POP PUNKS

These species are related to, or were spawned by, the advent of punk rock in the late 1970s. Though political leanings also may seem relevant, most experts consider similarity of musical taste and all that follows [i.e., fashion, habitat, etc.] to be most paramount to this grouping.

PUNK ROCKERS

REBELLIUM OSTENTATIA

LIBERTY SPIKES

CONTINENTAL
FLAIR

BLACK
LEATHER

PLAID

FIGURE 1
THE CRUSTY
PUNK

PUNK ROCKERS

Male
EXTERIOR: Skinny black or plaid pants (possibly with bondage straps); band T-shirt; fuzzy striped sweater; leather jacket (painted arms and back); bomber jacket with patches; flight jacket; Dr. Martens; Converse sneakers.
PLUMAGE: Mohawk or spikes.
ACCESSORIES: Studded belt or bondage belt with round hooks.

Female
EXTERIOR: Creepers (leopard print, velvet, plain black); bomber jacket with patches.

Both Sexes
VOICE: Guttural croaking often accompanied by snarled upper lip.

Though starved for attention, Punk Rockers do not take kindly to observation. *If confronted, sneer and spit to blend in. Avoid conservative hairstyles or casual sportswear.* A heavily tattooed and otherwise ornamented species, Punks derive their regimented and often predictable look by mixing the styles of early punk bands [e.g., The Ramones' leather jackets and striped shirts, The Clash's silk-screened T-shirts, The Sex Pistols' safety pins, etc.] with vintage sex shop attire [i.e., bondage and fetish gear, Malcolm McLaren's and Vivienne Westwood's early designs, etc.].

Though based largely on working-class fantasies of social rebellion, the species currently boasts an increasingly middle-class, suburban demographic. Even so, these Hipsters are generally bred in broken-home environments and exhibit a decidedly outcast disposition.

Also of note is Tiffen's Conjecture, an adage which provides for the possibility that Punk Rock Girls may be more hard core than their male counterparts. It states specifically that, despite gender-equitable difficulty, it is much crazier and "bad-assed" for a female to stroll down a city street sporting a Mohawk than it is for a male.

Origin of the Species:

Punks have perhaps the most densely convoluted history of all our Hipsters. One could spend years researching this species alone, though such an endeavor is not recommended. Suffice to say that the species first crawled out of the stadium, as it were, in 1976–77. Born out of general disaffection with both the popular music scene (stadium rock, concert theatrics, big tours, promotion) and society at large (Carter/Reagan/Thatcher-era politics), the original Punks were mainly noted for general ugliness and lack of musicianship.

Politics:

Like the Lazy (*Unemploydius Slothum*), Punk Rockers symbolically rebel against the norms of society, especially the ultimate evil: a 9 to 5 corporate work ethic. They purportedly advocate working for the community or the good of society, but oppose working for money [*see* the Dole]. Punks praise individuality, help those around them, and refuse to stab people in the back (though stabbing people in the Chelsea Hotel is encouraged).

Domestic specimens became more political and herd-oriented during the 1980s, a paradigm shift which resulted in the formulation of the Do It Yourself (DIY) credo. Intended as a reaction against the national media, DIY began as a simple, alternative method of keeping the Punk community informed and led eventually to such triumphs as Zines [i.e., shoddily produced homemade periodicals] and independent record labels.

Gender Roles:

Though Groupies have been, and will no doubt remain, an integral part of the scene, females often manage to contribute in a meaningful way, and not just attractive specimens like Deborah Harry [e.g., Patti Smith]. Women often work as publicists or producers, run labels, and produce Zines. There has also, in recent years, been a mass female migration to "the pit," rugged terrain reserved for the acts of slam-dancing (now termed "moshing") and stage-diving.

Pharmaceuticals:

The spectacle of the drunken Punk is, though ubiquitous, still very good for a laugh. Heroin, once the drug of choice and preferred means of death of many Punks, has recently fallen somewhat out of favor, a decline attributed as much to the drug's somewhat offputting lethal capabilities as to the general demographic shift toward a more pop-friendly makeup (specimens new to the scene are less likely to experiment with hard drugs). Similarly, the once-beloved practices of sniffing glue and huffing gasoline are passé to the modern Punk. Beer remains a huge element [e.g., Miller Genuine Draft, Pabst, Heineken, Guinness, Budweiser], while whiskey, scotch, and rum are also favorites.

Appeal, Ultimately:

Punk rock is a cry of the wild: a danceable surrogate for alternate, more destructive expressions of rage. These Hipsters, owing to their often tempestuous larval years, yearn for a self-contained theatre for release of their pent-up aggression. Most specimens exhibit a good deal of leftover teen angst, though unlike the whiny, sex-themed alienation preferred by Indie Rockers [*see* entry], theirs is more often the result of damaging familial situations [i.e., alcoholic, abusive, broken-home scenarios, etc.].

Related Species:

Given the species' status as disaffected youths blessed with fabulous fashion sense, the fact that these Hipsters have spawned several less substantive species is of little surprise. Two prominent examples are noted below:

CRUSTY PUNKS (*Nonhygenia Freeloadum*)—Something of a Punk Rocker/Hippie hybrid [*see* entry], these Hipsters are thoroughly reviled and disavowed by both. A filthy and repugnant species, Crusties are not particularly recommended for observation. However, their penchant for urban street begging makes avoidance practically impossible [Figure 1]. *Their entreaties should be ignored; move briskly.* In addition, these cretins are fevered proponents of an abhorrent residential opportunism known as "squatting." Effectively a communal form of responsibility shirking, squatting allows Crusties the opportunity to indulge both the Punk's DIY ethos and the Hippie's flair for dramatic activism. Free from the burdens of rent and taxes, they are able to pursue a quixotic existence of carpentry, heroin abuse, and potluck vegan dining.

POP PUNKS (*Teenybopperia Oneeightytwom*)—Also referred to as "Mall Punks," these Hipsters are noted mainly for their ability to co-opt the general Punk motif while draining it of any social, political, or economic import. Comprised primarily of middle class, suburban youngsters, the species excels at hair dyeing and crafting Punk-esque ditties with Top 40 radio appeal [e.g., Simple Plan, Good Charlotte, Sum 41, et al.].

Habitat:
Though not officially endangered, the Punk's natural terrain has recently suffered extensive environmental degradation. Encroaching forces such as hunting and persecution, land-claim issues, tourism, and the introduction of nonnative species [*see* Corporate Hipsters] are among the factors presently threatening the species. Such formerly pristine terrain as Coney Island High, Tramps, and The Wetlands (all in NYC), as well as The Rathskeller (a.k.a. "The Rat," in Boston) have already been completely depleted.

In Cincinnati, OH:
THE WARNER HOUSE *(344 Warner Avenue)*—This "subterranean cellar" is perfect for those who like to "sweat" and drink from "plastic cups" while listening to "hellishly" amateur punk rock. A "miserable" "anti"-bar complete with "disgusting" bathrooms, midwestern "homos" trying "desperately" to "offend," and girls who "couldn't show their putrid faces on King's Road," this basement venue offers less fun than a "cold winter with no jobs."

In Minneapolis, MN:

FIRST AVENUE & 7TH STREET ENTRY *(701 First Avenue North)*—Made famous by Prince's *Purple Rain*, this two-story club features a "dispossessed and wounded" décor scheme that's "horrible" and an "eclectic" concert schedule that leaves many regulars saying "what the bloody hell?" Be sure to avoid the "superficial trappings" of those "hip-hop nutters" in the main room, who are "more miserable than Labour."

In New York, NY:

CBGB *(315 Bowery)*—"Joey Ramone shat here" boast patrons of this East Side, historically registered hole in the wall with drink specials "perfectly calibrated to the Dole." Though cultural significance wanes, the cavernous basement area is still perfect for "eyeing birds" and getting "pissed," though some complain "that arsehole" working the door is "pure bollocks."

In Philadelphia, PA:

TATTOOED MOM'S *(530 South Street)*—Tell the "full of shite" "Hippie cunts" who populate South Street to "screw off"; this two-story bar is worth a look, especially for a jukebox which inspires "total social chaos." Impressionable "college chicks" are on hand to "have a bunk up" with, and even the "nastiest bastards" are sure to appreciate the general lack of "blood and confusion."

SKINHEADS

RAMBUNCTIUM DEFENSIVA

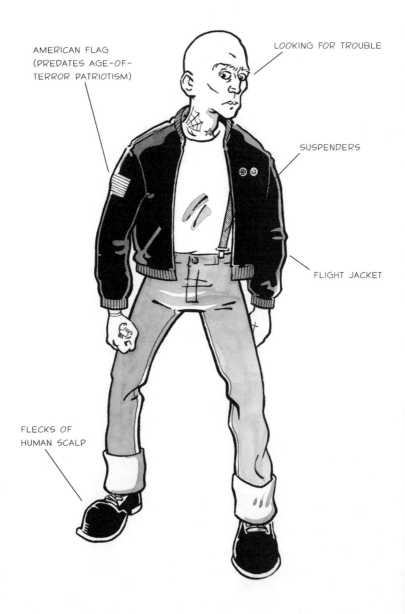

AMERICAN FLAG
(PREDATES AGE-OF-
TERROR PATRIOTISM)

LOOKING FOR TROUBLE

SUSPENDERS

FLIGHT JACKET

FLECKS OF
HUMAN SCALP

SKINHEADS

Male
EXTERIOR: Brown or black, tight "grandpa" cap; Fred Perry white shirt with black stripes on collar and sleeves (tucked in); tight, straight-leg, light or bleach-spotted Levi's (worn high on waist, cuffed 2 inches); black, high steel-toed Dr. Martens boots (top meets cuff precisely, laces around ankle).
ACCESSORIES: Suspenders ("braces").
PLUMAGE: Shaved (not completely).
MARKINGS: Heavily tattooed.

Female
EXTERIOR: Short, black mid-thigh skirt with flat pleats; little white bobby socks; low Dr. Martens boots; Fred Perry shirt (red or black).
PLUMAGE: Chelsea-style haircut.
MARKINGS: Light makeup, ear piercings.

kinheads can be dangerous to approach and have even developed the term "aggro" as evolutionary shorthand for their periodic and somewhat tiresome bursts of aggression. They exhibit a gang mentality similar to lesser *Graecus* species, notably Ex-Frats [*see* entry]: males are often rowdy, heavily reliant on hop-based alcoholic beverages, fanatically obsessed with sports, and territorial in regard to females. As with Straight-Edgers [*see* entry], these Hipsters find that a predetermined ideology offers quite a refreshing break from autonomous thought.

Origins of the Species:
The species was first observed crawling out of the storied primordial Hipster soup of late 1960s London, England. An offshoot of Mods [*see* entry], these Hipsters streamlined the frilly fashion and psychedelic

overtones inherent to said dandified specimens, most likely as a result of financial considerations.*

In reaction to slumming middle-class Punks [*see* entry], certain forward-thinking specimens created a determinedly crude form of street punk rock, termed "Oi!" after the Cockney slang for "hello." Oi! is decidedly angry and features an emphasis on heavy guitars, rat-tat-tat marching drumbeats, and football chant choruses [e.g., The Business, The Last Resort, Cockney Rejects, Sham 69, Cock Sparrer, The Templars, et al.].

Disposition:

Skinheads are quite fond of physical altercation and will not hesitate to clash over issues concerning females ("birds"), territory, respect, or bands/music. They rarely find simple fisticuffs sufficient; obsessed with weaponry, these Hipsters count brass knuckles, guns, knives, steel-toed Dr. Martens, and rock-filled socks among their favored instruments. Given such activity, these Hipsters often find themselves the recipients of state-sponsored incarceration, and, in fact, most specimens have spent time behind bars or, at the very least, embroiled in some sort of trouble with the law.

Breeds:

Unlike other species, which may exhibit distinctions of a semifrivolous or purely aesthetic nature, the following represent rigidly dissimilar types in terms of ideology. Much of Skinhead culture may be interpreted as a clash between the following:

TRADS—Short for "traditional," these Non-Racist Skins constitute the largest and most prevalent, if low-profile, breed. As Trad Skins have been completely overshadowed, in terms of popular recognition, by the minority Racist Skins [*see* below], some experts speculate that these Hipsters possess the most incompetent PR representation of all species.

*Remnants of this period remain, as some Skinheads have retained a strong attachment to perhaps the Mods' most recognizable urban accoutrement, the Italian motorized scooter [e.g., Vespa and Lambretta].

SHARPS or ARA SKINS—A highly politicized breed, these Hipsters are actively antiracist, and, in fact, their names derive from the movements to which they swear allegiance [viz., Skinheads Against Racial Prejudice, Anti-Racist Action]. Highly proactive, these Skins have been observed, for example, counterdemonstrating at Ku Klux Klan rallies.

BONEHEADS or NAZI SKINS—The most vile and problematic of all Hipsters, this parasitic breed has managed to thoroughly co-opt the entire aesthetic of a previously established species and has done so so thoroughly as to largely obscure the very existence of its host, a phenomenon otherwise unobserved in nature. In other words, Skinheads as a whole have become falsely synonymous with Bonehead politics. As the media makes no distinction between Boneheads and Trads, Skins are usually considered racist across the board. This breed is excessively violent. Observers, particularly those named Bernstein, are urged *to exercise extreme caution.*

Sexuality; Gender Roles:

Though a highly macho species, female specimens not only exist but are treated largely as equals. They are appropriately tough and tend to associate with non-Skinhead females only rarely. These Hipsters can be quite confrontational, and violence is sometimes common.

While actual sexual congress with a Skinhead should be attempted only by the most seasoned of observers, those who have undertaken such field study have reported something of a surprisingly traditional mating habit.

Plumage:

As a species literally defined by hairstyle, these Hipsters are extremely specific in regard to follicle manipulation. Males instinctually employ anything between a #4 and #1 crop [indicating shaver settings] in order to achieve the desired look.

Female Skins are notorious for exhibiting the most unattractive hairstyles in the entire Hipster Kingdom. Styles are limited to two: the Feather Cut or the Chelsea. Feather Cuts generally feature 3 to 5 inches of hair on top, with long bangs and fringe. The more popular Chelsea [Figure 1] typically involves a #4 to #1 crop accented by long (sometimes dyed) bangs, fringe, and optional pièce de résistance, the mullet back. The Chelsea is highly regarded by experts for its mysterious ability to thoroughly obscure even the most attractive of specimens.

FIGURE 1: THE CHELSEA

Habitat:

Due to their fringe status, tracking this species can prove quite difficult. One would think that, say, a simple Internet search for "Oi! Shows" might yield the desired fruitful results. Not so. In fact, some frustrated would-be observers have been known to ruin entire weekends staring desperately at their laptops. This being the case, acquiring a research assistant or intern is highly, highly recommended, if one possesses the means.

In Boston, MA:

GILLETTE STADIUM PARKING LOT *(One Patriot Place, Foxborough)*— The New England Revolution has been known to "kick Khyber" at this brand-new venue featuring ample space to "crack skulls," "kitchen sink" some "Britney," or "stomp" a few "oily rags." Whether you call it "football" or "soccer," there's no denying that this sport is "second rate."

In Chicago, IL:

GUNTHER MURPHY'S *(1638 West Belmont Avenue)*—Grab a few "pints" of "laugh and titter" and put on your "affected brogue" at this authentic "rub-a-dub" where "leprechauns are considered unmentionable" and most patrons appreciate the "whites only" clientele. Though the bands are sometimes "Jackson Pollocks," it's never been so much fun being an "all-time loser."

In Portland, OR:

THE MATADOR *(1967 West Burnside Street)*—So cool you "almost forget you're in Oregon," this long-standing lounge is a great place to "top hat" with your "chinas" over some "Louise Ruse." Saturday's "Britpop" night is highly recommended for those in the mood for an "apple crumble" with some "effeminate little gravel and grits." Locals recommend a little "Posh & Becks" in the "Gary Glitter."

In St. Louis, MO:

THE CREEPY CRAWL *(412 North Tucker Boulevard)*—A real piece of "pony," "lemon squeezers" and their "twist and twirls" flock to this raw, grungy institution to "chant" mindlessly ("Oi! Oi! Oi!") and have a few "giraffes." Live local music is the main draw, but some discerning patrons feel that all "these Punk wankers" are "worse than Jews."

STRAIGHT-EDGE

HIPTO BESQUARUM

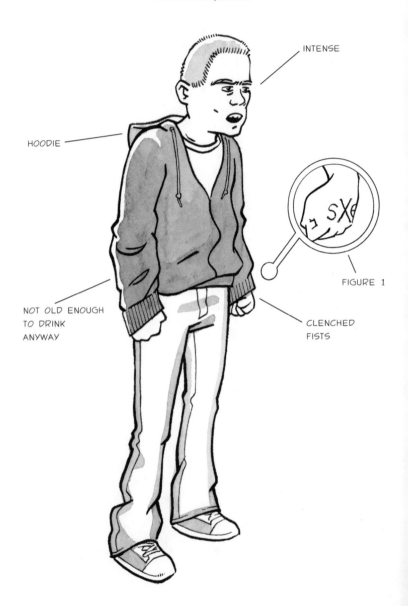

INTENSE

HOODIE

NOT OLD ENOUGH
TO DRINK
ANYWAY

CLENCHED
FISTS

FIGURE 1

STRAIGHT-EDGE

EXTERIOR: Varies—wide-legged pants; running shoes; baggy khakis; polo shirt; band or Straight-Edge–themed T-shirt.
ACCESSORIES: Wallet chain; backpack; homework.
MARKINGS: "X" on paw.
LIFE SPAN: Three years.

xtremely self-aware (and even self-labeled), these Hipsters have managed to reinterpret the very concept of Hipness in order to lend some countercultural cachet to a lifestyle both utterly devoid of youthful trappings and, indeed, identical to that preferred by such non-Hip specimens as Squares, Nerds, Mommy's Boys, Pansies, Bible Students, Goody Two-Shoeses, and Chickens.

Their lifestyle is a rigorous one, and is not recommended for those with weak spirits, strength of character, or lust for life. Specimens who have chosen to adopt this ethos are branded for purposes of identification, usually on the paw [Figure 1]. *They are thus quite suited for observation.* Their symbol, an homage to the "X" once used by bouncers at all-age Punk shows to distinguish minors not able to legally purchase alcohol, is actually pronounced "Sexy," a fact both incredibly ironic and slightly pathetic.

Straight-Edgers are often Born-Again Hipsters. That is, transgressions of the past [i.e., one-night stands, alcoholic revelry, joy] no longer matter; all is conveniently forgiven once one has been accepted by the flock. There exists, however, a certain minority, sometimes referred to as "Absolute Straight-Edge," which has purportedly never participated in any frowned-upon activities.

Comprised largely of suburban, middle-class, white males, the species tends to skew quite young [i.e., 12–20].

Philosophy:

Though difficult to fathom, these Hipsters have purposefully abandoned such activities as smoking, drinking alcohol, doing drugs, and casual sex.* Most experts do not believe that the species is, at present, opposed also to such devilish accoutrements as electricity or motorcars. Recently, the species has also come to embrace the practice of vegetarianism and even, in some hysterical cases, veganism. It is here that the species crosses ideological paths with the similarly minded Activists [*see* entry] and adopts a semimilitant countenance. Apparently, their pro-animal, PETA-friendly politics require a level of confrontational vigilance that their puritanical abstinence does not.

Straight-Edgers often exhibit a crudely expressed superiority complex. Unable to come completely to terms with their limited social options and frightened by the possibility of personal blandness, many specimens become curiously convinced of their own empowerment and distinction.

Origin of the Species:

An offshoot of Punk Rockers [*see* entry], Straight-Edge was born amid the Washington, D.C., hard-core scene of the early 1980s as something of a rejection of the general hedonism and self-destruction inherent to this scene at that time. The term "Straight-Edge" itself was coined by the seminal band Minor Threat in their song of the same name.[†] This track, along with the similarly themed "Out of Step," laid down much of the original Straight-Edge ethos.

Disposition:

The species can at times be excessively aggressive, though such activity is largely limited to the dance floor (specifically in the terrain designated as the "mosh pit"). In said environments, these Hipsters exhibit a

*Due to their practically identical philosophies, it should come as small surprise that certain specimens become entangled in Hare Krishna tenets (no gambling, intoxicants, meat, or illicit sex). By achieving such synergy, these Hipsters are able to assume a spiritual identity posthaste and with utmost convenience.

[†] Minor Threat's leader, Ian MacKaye, is something of a Hipster progenitor. His subsequent band, Embrace, is often credited with spawning emo, a weepy hard-core/indie rock subgroup, while his current outfit, Fugazi, remain the torchbearers of latter-day Do It Yourself (DIY) ethos.

strong penchant for violent physical expression. Their instinctual need to thus comport themselves is matched, conveniently, by an innate fondness for labeling. An abbreviated listing of favored dances follows:

THE WINDMILL—Similar to childish approximations of fisticuffs; arms rotating 360 degrees wildly backwards, fists clenched, while skipping side to side.

FLOORPUNCHING—Literal definition applies.

THE WALL OF DEATH—Comprised of numerous, arm-locked specimens who, moving as one, sweep through innocent Hipsters in their path.

Habitat:

During the Straight-Edge heyday (ca. 1988), Washington, D.C., was recognized as the most pristine environment in which to observe the species' anachronistic and amusingly quaint way of life. As the scene flourished, these Hipsters spread to virtually all urban terrain. Today, Straight-Edgers may be found wherever underage kids, or the painfully dull, yearn to "party." Clubs featuring high concentrations of hard-core concerts remain the prospective observers' best bet as far as this species is concerned.

In Los Angeles, CA:
THE SMELL *(247 South Main Street)*—Due to its convenient "lack of liquor license" and "hard-core" back alley entrance, this "positive" concert space is regarded as a "superior" venue to all but the best "American Legion halls." Traditionally small crowds leave plenty of space to "mosh," "thrash," or execute the occasional "stage dive."

In Providence, RI:
MET CAFÉ *(130 Union Street)*—"Gosh darn," this club is "the poop." Show some "unity" by holding a booth for your friends or "flirt, but not too heavily" with "cute girls from RISD." "Bust it up" to the live bands, but be careful not to "skank" in the "pit." The bar is great for "carving Xs into," though unfortunately they don't offer "pitchers of O'Douls."

In Rochester, NY:

THE BUG JAR *(219 Monroe Avenue)*—"It's too bad I don't drink," because "these $2 Mickeys work perfectly with my allowance," lament visitors to this "crucial" alternative music venue noted for its cutting "edge" sound and a kitschy 1950s décor scheme as out-of-date as "my stunted views on human sexuality." Bring your whole "crew"; this place is "massive."

In San Diego, CA:

CHE CAFÉ *(UC, San Diego)*—"Drop me off around the block, please" plead regulars at this "rad" all-ages venue. Grab something off the "Zine rack" and settle in with some "all you can eat vegan delicacies" before taking in a show or discussing the "evils of masturbation." Beware of "posers"; some say "that guy over there in the Dead Kennedys T-shirt" has been observed "littering."

The *Graecus* Family

Hipsters of this family are noted for their bovinelike conformity and lack of "edge." Though not mindless per se, they struggle with personal autonomy and seek comfort in the safety of numbers. While exhibiting some deviation from the norm, Men Who Lunch are generally grouped herein due to their proclivity to, if enrolled at a university, engage in some variance of either Greek or Secret Society life.

L ike their male counterparts [see Ex-Frats], this species' period of undergraduate gestation serves as the armature for their subsequent, graduation-induced forays into the "real world." While mainstream in appearance, these Hipsters do exhibit some prevailing sense of trend; today's low-rider jeans are merely yesterday's tight black pants. Considerable energy is expended keeping abreast (no pun intended) of what one should be wearing. Luckily, up-to-the-minute updates are available via the Internet [e.g., www.dailycandy.com], as are economical means of acquisition [e.g., www.nysale.com].

Herd Mentality:

An inborn herd instinct, long ago suppressed by most non-*Graecus* species, is thought responsible for the Alpha Female's willingness to embrace Greek life. The well-documented appeal of safety in numbers is in this instance further compounded by a desperate need to assemble, at university, an approximation of secondary school cliquishness. Fortunately, the species' unique and instinctual cry for help, termed "rushing," is usually rewarded with an instant social life without necessitating the untidy and tiring process of actually having to go out and "meet people." Only the most undesirable cretins are left unclaimed after this intricate and pagan process. Said specimens are left by the wayside, either to die or graduate with honors.

The process of the "rush" differs slightly from herd to herd, though most involve singing, dimmed lights, lit candles, heart-to-heart discourses on sorority life, alcohol, black costumes, and brutal evaluation.

Similar in form to a slave auction, these multitiered events are more hotly contested than an NFL draft.

Mating Rituals:

An Alpha Female's housemates, or "Sisters," function mainly as sexual enablers. Prevailing logic dictates that "As long as everyone else is sleeping around, why shouldn't I?" In fact, the sluttiest girl in the Sorority House is often used as a point of reference: "Well, at least I'm not as bad as Jackie." In some extreme cases, baskets of condoms are left around the House as gestures of goodwill.

Two contradictions neatly illustrate the species' intricate web of sexual deviation and denial. They are as follows:

1. Despite their being regarded as nice, normal, sweet, mainstream girls and future wives, members of this species tend to be a million times more debauched than any seemingly more risqué breed [*see* Punk Rockers, Butch/Femmes, Goths].

2. Outward expressions of sexuality are stifled despite House-sanctioned promiscuity behind closed doors, e.g., the girl reprimanded for topless dancing who replies, "But Susie, Kimmy, and Lexi double-teamed the Phi Gams last night" [said girl was summarily expelled from the House].

The species' intricate mating dance (a delicate combination of alcohol, lapsed judgment, and low self-esteem) culminates in a morning-after stumble toward home, referred to colloquially as the "Walk of Shame" [Figure 1].

In some instances, Alpha Females have been known to become socially entangled with a non-*Graecus* male, though the practice remains rare (particularly in the Deep South).

FIGURE 1

Post-Collegiate Migration:

Following college graduation, Alpha Females typically follow one of two routes: immediate move to the suburbs and marriage, or career-oriented and temporary move to a large city. Given the species' insatiable appetite for matchmaking, the former is more common. Mixers, pre-bars, after hours, house parties, et al., function as creative excuses to couple and prey upon a young girl's vision of marriage and happiness. The infamous "Screw Your Sisters" event is the collegiate matchmaker's Holy Grail [described, below, by a specimen whom we shall call "Krissy"]:

> Screw Your Sisters is such pussy dating. It gives girls the opportunity to invite guys they have been to [*sic*] scared to approach out to a party. What happens is [that] sisters draw each other's names and invite dates for that sister. So let's say I draw Tiffany. I'll ask Tiffany who would you like to be screwed with? She'll give me a list and then I'll contact those guys. Sometimes you only invite one guy, sometimes more (to cover your bases). From there everyone meets at the party and girls pretend to be shocked to find out that Frat Boy Tom Smith was invited for them ... meanwhile they have a shrine to him back at the Sorority House.

Having spent four years equating sexual conquest with life success, it is unsurprising that many Alpha Females choose to settle down immediately with their college sweethearts.

"Let's Keep in Touch" Taken Literally:

Despite the Alpha Females' lack of physical proximity to the Sorority House, much of their social culture involves both frequent appraisals of goings-on back at school as well as fevered attempts at reunions large and small. Newsletters are written, printed, and distributed to each House-specific circle on a regular, periodic basis. It is with great interest that Alpha Females debate the merits of this year's incoming Rushers and keep track of nationwide get-togethers. City-dwelling Alpha Females are particularly keen to schedule Happy Hours, at which the consumption of alcohol and the wearing of tight shirts have been observed and, in some cases, exploited.

Weddings are the mother of all Sorority House reunions. These fantastical and storied affairs represent the culmination of feverish Husband Hunting and the well-deserved reward for endless nights spent in solitary, ornamental prepping.

Independent Thought as Social Liability:

The herd is strong-willed and dissenters are shunned and not flirted with. Alpha Females have gone so far as to develop coded language for those choosing to live life on their own terms: "God Damned Independents ($\Gamma\Delta I$)." This marks the first time in nature that independent thought has been officially bastardized.

Cat Fight!:

This species raises infighting to an art form. In the girl-slap-girl world of the Alpha Female, anyone not present is ripe for commenting derisively upon. The bitchiness is often quite elegant; familiar yet unnamed females are routinely identified by their known involvement in unflattering events [i.e., "Look, there's the girl who double-teamed her professor and TA"]. Furthermore, in a sophisticated bit of evolutionary shorthand, Alpha Females trade heavily in nicknames, such as the time-honored "Horse Face."

Habitat:

These Hipsters possess no real social interests of their own and will congregate in whichever terrain the male of the species prefers.

In New York, NY:
CLUB AT TURTLE BAY *(236 East 47th Street)*—"Hookups" are practically "guaranteed" at this midtown homage to *Animal House.* Leaving "empty-handed" is not only "unheard of" but "really, really embarrassing." Even "that troll" who "wouldn't have made it past pledge week" is going to go home with someone. "Jim told me her tits sag." "Slut."

SUTTON PLACE *(1015 Second Avenue)*—"Three stories of crap," this post-collegiate Happy Hour theme park features a cigar lounge full of "obnoxious, coughing, yet kind of cute" boys, DJs spinning "classics" like "that Vitamin C graduation song," a video wall for "sports," and a lovely rooftop perfect for "jumping off of" when the crowd becomes "unbearable." The music is "really loud," forcing patrons to practically "stick his tongue in my ear," while the food tastes "better than semen."

In Philadelphia, PA:
CHEMISTRY NIGHTSPOT *(4100 Main Street)*—Put on your "sluttiest" outfit, 'cause "girls rule" at this dance club populated with "guys studying to be doctors" who "go to the gym, too." Be prepared to "par-tay" and keep in mind that even though baseball caps are not allowed, "he'll hopefully wear one on our second date." Regulars claim "that bartender thinks she's so hot."

In Washington, D.C.:
CARPOOL *(4000 Fairfax Drive, Arlington)*—Drive your "Civic" to this auto-themed pool bar that reminds locals of "that road trip we took to Savannah for St. Patrick's Day junior year, remember that?" Boys in "cute" "Abercrombie T-shirts" are fun to "flirt" with in between "darts," but the barbecue, beer, and jukebox "with my prom song on it!" are the real attractions.

CORPORATE HIPSTERS/HIP BY NIGHT

TRENDIDIA NOCTURNUM

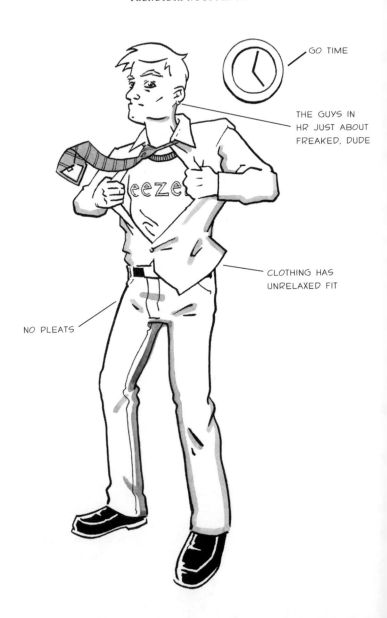

GO TIME

THE GUYS IN HR JUST ABOUT FREAKED, DUDE

CLOTHING HAS UNRELAXED FIT

NO PLEATS

CORPORATE HIPSTERS

EXTERIOR: Muscular, husky build. Dress similar to AlternaBoys or Indie Rockers. Denim jeans; trendy sandals; chunky dress shoes; vintage button-up shirts; tight solid T-shirt (blue, gray, or black).
ACCESSORIES: Sunglasses (indoors or out); garish hat; sneer.
MARKINGS: Tattoos and piercings rare.
VOICE: Excitable, incessant chattering.

This species is noted for its mysterious ability to reside on the cutting edge of countercultural trendiness despite staunch pro-corporate and anticreative leanings. As role players and mimics, the species knows no equal. To the casual observer, Corporate Hipsters may at many times appear authentically alternative. They spend considerable effort, energy, and most importantly cash perpetuating this ruse and have grown quite adept at it.

The species funds its stylish lifestyle through a lifetime of noncreative and uninteresting work. As a result, these cretins are able to afford better goods and services than the actual Hipsters whom they strive to emulate. Like AlternaBoys [see entry], Corporate Hipsters have been greatly abetted in their mission by the advent of web design, a profession which allows them to remain employed by conglomerates, yet in a pseudoartistic, often "freelance" capacity.

As tourists in two distinct worlds (Corporate/Hip), they belong wholly to neither. Lacking the talent and courage necessary for pursuing a career in the arts, while at the same time retaining the delusions of creativity which obstruct a wholesale integration into office life, these Hipsters are relegated to a murky, confused, and ultimately pathetic mental state. As a result, they can be incredible bores at both parties and dinner gatherings.

The species is able to transform itself from Corporate to Hip at will. While experts estimate that this metamorphosis generally occurs between 5:00 and 5:30 P.M., Monday through Friday, the process has never actually been observed in nature.

Identification:

As noted above, the species appears Hip by assuming the aesthetics of certain legitimately Hip species, particularly those generally less flamboyant [see AlternaBoys, DJs, Indie Rockers, Starving Artists]. The seasoned observer need not be fooled. Several specific character traits reliably give the species away for what it truly is. They are:

1. An Ex-Frat–like love of weekends [see entry].

2. A penchant for self-promotion and resultant dismal creative advice giving [e.g., suggesting topics for a writer to pursue].

3. An inability to recognize the point at which one may be too accessorized.

4. An insistence on having the last word, regardless of expertise or even familiarity with the subject [e.g., publishing, politics, urbanization, infrastructure, cinema, et al.].

5. A continual cycle of self-rationalization and explanation [e.g., listing the various reasons why they have decided not to quit their job to pursue the arts].

6. A loud, booming voice.

7. Muscles.

8. An inability to compromise.

Mating Rituals:

In order to ensnare an agreeable female, Corporate Hipsters troll pools of slightly younger, noncreative Career Girls.* Often fresh off post-

---

*The species is overwhelmingly male. Female specimens may exist, though remain largely undocumented.

Graecus relationships, these victims are easily fooled and wooed by the comparably non-Frattish behavior of the Corporate Hipster, who treats them to a whirlwind of expensively chic and culturally advantageous outings [e.g., sushi dinners, outdoor concerts, Pygmalion-esque museum trips, etc.]. The female's simple relief at the break in her vicious cycle of sports bar alcohol slinging and late-night vomiting leads to a fairly high success rate.

Habitat:

By day, Corporate Hipsters are best viewed in well-populated lunch-break terrain. However, in such environments they are quite physically indistinguishable from normal Corporate Types.

By night, the species will only tread upon acknowledged trendy terrain. They consult entertainment guides [e.g., *TimeOut New York*] and the hip media [e.g., *Vice* magazine] with a fervor bordering on the religious and will only consent to grace an establishment once it has been identified as groundbreakingly hip.

In New York, NY:

DINER *(85 Broadway Street, Brooklyn)*—"Put this on my company card," request regulars at this Williamsburg hot spot who "apologize for being late, the train was horrible." Slip into your new "vintage military cadet shirt" before feasting on "burgers better than anywhere in Midtown," smoking a few "cigs," and regaling the table with "highlights from my new résumé." While most enjoy "monopolizing the conversation," some "can't believe they stuck me in the back room."

VOID *(16 Mercer Street)*—This "chill" lounge is dark enough to "publicly grope my girlfriend" while "explaining" the "experimental videos" being projected on the wall-size screen that's "bigger than my ego." Though some have "thought about making films," most are content to just "play a few games of 'Pac-Man' " and "critique the DJ" before "taking off" for some "late-night sushi."

In Boston, MA:

ENORMOUS ROOM *(567 Massachusetts Avenue, Cambridge)*—More comfortable than "the Aeron Chair in my office," this loftlike space is great for "letting off a little steam" after a "really nasty board meeting" or "second-guessing" some of "Abel Ferrara's weaker efforts." Regulars enjoy the "performance art," though some feel "I did better work in my freshman improv elective."

DELUX CAFÉ *(100 Chandler Street)*—"I used to come here with this French girl from college," claim "obnoxious" patrons of this bar/restaurant that's "pretty decent, I suppose" and "definitely much better than that place you guys wanted to try." The food, though delicious, reminds some of "my parents' country club." Presentation, however, never fails to impress, as the chef is "almost as creative as selling short/buying long."

EX-FRATS

HOMOEROTICUM MISOGYNYSTICA

BRAND LOYALTY

SOMEWHERE
BETWEEN TUCKED
AND UNTUCKED

BEER TANK

PLEATS

FIGURE 1

EX-FRATS

EXTERIOR: Business—Brooks Brothers dress shirt; long-sleeve polo (Eddie Bauer, Brooks Brothers, Banana Republic); pleated, black or dark-colored slacks with tapered cuffs; dark socks; black square-toe shoes (Kenneth Cole); leather coat; solid black belt with silver buckle. Casual—Floppy baseball cap or Abercrombie & Fitch visor; thin V-neck sweater over white T-shirt; crew neck sweater (with horizontal stripes) over white T-shirt; semicasual collared shirt (tucked in); fitted blue jeans or khaki pants; J. Crew flip-flops or open toe sandals; beachwear.

ACCESSORY: Sony Sport Walkman (for commute).

VOICE: Series of staccato notes, following pattern of *beer-beer-beer-tits-tits-beer-beer-beer.*

E x-Frats are unique among our Hipsters in that they are unable to reproduce sexually. Instead, the species must recruit new members at the collegiate level. New recruits are branded to distinguish among tribes, or "Houses," often with a Grecian triptych. Outsiders are shunned, ridiculed, and sprayed with beer.

Much of the culture centers on an obsession with glory days gone by. While outwardly adopting a grown-up, businesslike persona, Ex-Frats yearn for the debauchery of youth, a debauchery revisited annually at the requisite Summer Beach House, often located far afield [e.g., the Hamptons, the Jersey Shore, Newport, Panama City, Myrtle Beach, Dewey Beach, Cape Cod, et al.]. When confronted by Ex-Frats in such terrain, *drink to fit in. If crossing your legs is a must, do not go further than ankle upon knee.*

Loafer and Wallet Disease:

Ex-Frats may carry Loafer and Wallet Disease, which behavioral scientists have classified as a Pressurized Ale Dispenser Withdrawal Affliction (PADWA). Owing to postcollegiate cramped living spaces (ill-suited, as they are, to large drunken throngs), the species is often separated from its source of power, the keg of beer [Figure 1]. Unable to channel their aggressions through beer stands and funnels, Ex-Frats stricken with Loafer and Wallet Disease are inappropriately loud, unruly, and competitive at all public events. Sports bars, stadiums, and faux-Irish pubs are especially good environments for spotting PADWA-induced spectacles. The "street fight" is also popular, though less savagely contested than among other species [*see* Punks], since brawling in sensible shoes is an awkward and difficult business.

PADWA is transmitted through nostalgia. It poses no health risks to other species, though economic implications do exist [e.g., bouts of premature selling on floor of the Exchange, increased police presence outside sporting stadiums, replacement costs for smashed pint glasses, broken stools, etc.]. There is as yet no known cure, though some experts recommend quarantine. *Avoid entering conversations beginning with the phrase "Remember the time . . . ?" If this proves impossible, putting your ego aside is recommended. Yes, you did go to a safety school. Yes, you are queer. No, Joe Montana is not a better quarterback than Dan Marino. And so on.*

Often, PADWA outbreaks are accompanied or fueled by the music of Bruce Springsteen and Pearl Jam, though no known endorsement by said musicians has been made public.

Raison d'être; Pursuit of 19th Hole:
The possible existence of a 19th Hole looms large over the Ex-Frat's proverbial golf course of life. This 19th Hole is viewed as a Shangri-la, where the beer flows pure and cool, where baseball season never ends, where no boast is too big nor brow too low.

Outside of possessing a high-risk 401(k) plan, the species is relatively tame. Ex-Frats delight in celebrating the status quo and elevating mainstream, lowest-common-denominator thinking to its own ironic (to the observer) cachet. Also, constant intraspecies competition fuels much of the Ex-Frat's existence. From who makes more money to who has groped more women to who was at the office later last night to who has a cooler hometown, all topics are fair game for wagering. In fact, much of the species' infatuation with money stems from a primordial need to fund such bets. In order to keep up, most specimens pursue well-paying, if somewhat pedestrian, occupations [e.g., accounting, financial analysis, marketing, law, et al.].

Sexuality; Complexity of Sexual Orientation:
Males routinely condescend to members of the opposite sex, whom they consider inferior. Drunken liaisons and eventual "settling down" are tolerated, though the latter has been known to cause complications among male members of the herd. The platonic male/female relationship is practically unheard of and indeed frowned upon. When the sexes do mingle, only male-approved activities are permitted, thus the common spectacle of females staring absently at televised football.

That Ex-Frats are perhaps the most misogynistic of our Hipsters is interesting in light of the serious homoerotic overtones of the culture. Practically all males have seen each other naked on at least one occasion, often in a locker room or drunken stupor. In fact, many new recruits are "hazed" in a series of decidedly gay tests of will. One common ritual is known as "the Elephant Walk," in which Ex-Frats line up naked single file, each placing one thumb in the anus of the boy in front of him and the other thumb in his own mouth. They are then made to march around the room; any thumb dislodging from any anus resulting in a swapping of thumbs from mouth to anus and vice versa.

Related Hipster:
Certain specimens have been known to deviate from the tenets of officially recognized *Graecus* life. Once they successfully remove themselves from the herd, said Hipsters are technically categorized under the separate subcategory Ex-Frat Apologists (*Homoeroticum Repentiva*). Noted for an innate inability to reconcile themselves to their own pasts, these Hipsters exhibit the tendency to lobby consistently for acceptance by those disapproving of the Ex-Frat lifestyle. They are desperate to distinguish themselves as non-Frat Guys, despite overwhelming evidence

to the contrary. Their complex rationalizations can generally be categorized according to three main criteria:

1. The insistence that "everyone at my college rushed."

2. The insistence that "not everyone is like that."

3. The insistence that the specimen in question "stopped paying dues after sophomore year" and became, largely, "inactive."

Physically, these Hipsters present a distinctive mermanlike appearance. That is, most specimens retain, from the waist up, major Ex-Frat characteristics [i.e., baseball hats, collegiate T-shirts] while, from the waist down, highlight their new countercultural allegiances [i.e., Dickies, work pants, Western-style belt buckles, Dr. Martens].

Habitat:

Ex-Frat migratory patterns cover entire urban areas (excluding minority-rich zones), with heavy emphasis on corporate-friendly Happy Hour environments. Furthermore, they are indigenous to practically all terrain, both urban and otherwise.

In Boston, MA:
THE KELLS *(161 Brighton Avenue)*—"BC Rules!" claim patrons of this Irish-themed complex featuring "awesome kamikaze shots" and several "hot chicks I'd love to bang out." Authentic it isn't, though for ladies interested in being groped or guys who "don't mind a sausage party," this "sweaty" locale is "killer boots." Be forewarned, however, "only in Boston" do "faux-Irish" pubs actually charge a cover.

In New York, NY:
DOC WATSON'S *(1490 Second Avenue)*—The lovely back garden puts this Irish bar in a league of its own, though some complain that the setting is "gay." Guinness posters "like my Big Brother had" help create an air of comfort and style in which to "pound beers." The downstairs pool room is perfect for a quick game or "hand job," while the relatively intelligent clientele makes this Eastsider a "thinking man's kegger."

In Philadelphia, PA:
FLAT ROCK SALOON *(4301 Main Street, Manayunk)*—If you miss the heady days of "keg parties" and "passed-out chicks" but have come to reluctantly accept "my shitty job" and "prematurely" graying hair, this Manayunk staple is a perfect spot for "reuniting Greek-style" and "pounding" an eclectic selection of imported brews. "Wing night" is both "sweet" and a great way to "forget about the fact that I'm not married yet."

In Washington, D.C.:
ADAMS MILL BAR AND GRILL *(1813 Adams Mill Road NW)*—For the "chauvinist" with "refined tastes," this semi-upscale Happy Hour favorite is noted for its "dried flowers," "tastefully appointed" patio, and "that White House intern with an awesome rack." After a long day of "sexually harassing my secretary," settle in for a few "Miller Lites" and enjoy "the game."

MEN WHO LUNCH

GILDEDUM SUPERFLUOSA

ARISTOCRATIC CHIN

MASCULINE
(ANGLE OF WRIST
NOTWITHSTANDING)

LOAFERS
VALUED AT
MORE THAN
YOUR
NET WORTH

AT EASE

MEN WHO LUNCH

EXTERIOR: Physically fit; slighty Euro; slightly shiny button-down dress shirt (tight, tucked in, rolled to elbow); straight black pants; black shoes (never pointy or square) purchased at Juno.
ACCESSORIES: Obviously expensive belt (though no label à la Gucci buckle) with sterling buckle or similarly obnoxious flourish; rimless oval eyeglasses (titanium or black frames); Patek Philippe gold face watch with alligator band.
PLUMAGE: Styled hair (not overly done); possible hint of dishevelment.

E ngineered by their fabulously wealthy fathers, Men Who Lunch prove that human beings can exist who undermine the very fabric of what makes us civilized.

Due to the divine nature of their birthrights, these Hipsters remain legends in their own minds despite serving no tangible purpose. *Pointing this out is not recommended. If confronted, exaggerate your net worth.* Whether financiers, real estate developers, Hollywood producers, or titans of industry, this species' paterfamilias have worked hard to ensure their offspring a life of uninterrupted leisure. Every Dunhill cigarette they smoke is a fabulous affirmation of their self-worth and humanity. *Observe carefully and from a distance. The lifestyle is extremely attractive yet unattainable.*

The Old College Try:

Men Who Lunch find their origins, for the most part, in New York City or Los Angeles. They are bred at the finest prep schools [e.g., Dalton, Collegiate School, Horace Mann, et al.] before matriculation at the nation's foremost universities. Though some fellow students find their presence there to be as distasteful and undeserving as, say, the ace pitcher of the softball team's, Men Who Lunch are integral to the education system as it presently exists. The species simultaneously provides the bottom of the curve and the top of the endowment pile to our great colleges. In fact, many experts speculate that the poor kid from New Jersey would be unable to receive an *A* without the rich kid from New York getting a *D*. Similar to the Ex-Frat in size and appearance [*see* entry], MWL participate in Greek Life more for its Secret Society–like exclusivity than for its beer and broads brand of debauchery. The Frat House is the closest most specimens will ever come to the hallowed halls of a Masonic temple. They are sons of Masons, but not Masons themselves.

Lack of Masculinity:
To say that Men Who Lunch lack masculinity does not imply that they are somehow feminine, but that the very concept of masculinity is absent from their world. The very fact of their existence in society, contrary to the rest of civilization, places them above the need to assert themselves in roles assigned by others. Since there is no ambiguity regarding their sexual strength and domination, they feel no pressure to assert their masculinity. As a result, Men Who Lunch are free to indulge in and surround themselves with concerns and issues that could be regarded as less than masculine by males of most species. Personal upkeep and diet, for example, consume much of their time and effort [*see* below]. Also of interest is their continual debate concerning the worth and expertise of certain stylists.

Regimented Leisure:
Due to exclusivity of terrain, relatively little is known concerning the species' specific daily routine. It was long theorized that time simply floated by in a decidedly ad hoc style of leisure and indulgence, one day dissolving casually into the next. Recent advancements in the field, however, indicate that several events are actually scheduled daily. Kushner's Conjecture, presented below, represents current scientific speculation regarding this rare species' habits and routine:

A.M.

11:40 Meet Samantha for brunch.

P.M.

1:20 Telephone Mummy.

2:30 Dealer.

4:00 Shopping.

5:30 Manicure and massage.

Here the trail becomes faint, obscured by a practically impenetrable melange of velvet ropes, guest lists, secret after-hours parties, and membership-only clubs. Field researchers have yet to overcome their inherently paltry salaries and related lack of expense accounts and thus remain unable to operate in the aforementioned terrain, though Dr. Holly von Heintz, Professor Emeritus of Hipster Studies, UPenn, author of *Hipsters in the Mist*, and quite cute, has recently been propositioned by the scion of a prominent shipping magnate, so hopes remain high.

Database of the Privileged:
Men Who Lunch are the parasites of the bar scene. They select a locale, infest, draw crowds, suck out the life, and move on. The species consistently reinterprets just exactly what is "in" and what is "out" socially. MWL possess a keen sixth sense which alerts them to the precise moment, to within several seconds, when a band, bar, club, style, brand, hairstyle, color, restaurant, philosophy, drug, neighborhood, artist, stock, model, socialite, stylist, cocktail, automobile, etc., has become embarrassingly passé.

Habitat:
Pinning down the species' specific habitat is extremely difficult, for reasons described above [i.e., exclusivity and constant variation]. However, locales featuring particularly prohibitive financial requirements are extremely good places to begin. MWL may occasionally be spotted

in more casual terrain, as they enjoy slumming at movie theatres, malls, and live music venues. They have an incredible amount of time to kill, and after all one cannot lunch all day.

In Los Angeles, CA:

BLUE ON BLUE *(9400 West Olympic Boulevard, Beverly Hills)*—"Hold on, Mother, I need to order" note "Fred Segal"-clad patrons perusing the slightly "banal" menu at this poolside hotel eatery. Though some wish they'd brought their "trunks," others prefer "just sitting here with Brad" or poking "absently" at a "Caesar Salad" while "resigning myself" to a "ski weekend with Emily." The lounging starlets are hot enough to cut through even the most persistent "drug-fueled impotence," but beware wanna-be celebrity types who "I think used to clean our pool."

THE IVY *(113 North Robertson Boulevard)*—Grab your "usual table" and settle in for a few hours of "directionless lounging" at this quaint "power lunch" fave of those who "actually work." The practically shabby décor offers a refreshing counterpoint to hours spent "cooped up in my parent's beachfront mansion" while the fried seafood mega-platter provides "perfect" sustenance for a night spent "screwing the chauffeur's daughter."

In New York, NY:

BOND STREET *(6 Bond Street)*—Avoid the basement lounge, where "less fortunate" types gather to bask in the secondhand glow of this Pan-Asian hot spot's regular patrons. Send a drink over to "Leo's table" before settling in to discuss "tennis tomorrow" or debate the merits of "this new wax I've been using." The "stiff drinks" are a perfect antidote to "this horrifyingly dreary lunch with Father today."

THEO *(325 Spring Street)*—"Have you had a chance to see my pecs?" ask visitors to this West SoHo eatery where "my father's lawyer brokered the lease" and "those girls over there seem sort of fine, I guess." Whether meeting your "dealer" or "trying to remember what day of the week it is," the hearty, New American fare "looks nice" next to "my new tan."

The *Hedonistium* Family

TWO SPECIES:

1. EUROTRASH

2. RAVERS

These two seemingly disparate species are related by their primordial needs to party. Both are fond of loud dance music, pharmaceuticals, large gatherings, flashy accoutrements, and general deviance. Stylistically quite opposite, these Hipsters are nevertheless practically identical in function.

EUROTRASH

INFILTRATA MATERIALUM

NOT "INTO" GUYS FROM SOUTH JERSEY

RECEDING SEPTUM

NOT PURCHASED PERSONALLY

CHEST HAIR

BRAZILIAN WAX RUMORED

GAUDY WATCH (IN UNLIKELY CASE HE EVER HAS TO BE SOMEWHERE)

AMERICANS ARE SO FAT IT'S DISGUSTING

SHOES MADE OF SOMETHING HE WOULDN'T TOUCH ALIVE

GAULOISE

EUROTRASH

Male
EXTERIOR: Armani or Versace button-down dress shirt (tucked in);
dress pants; black shoes; black socks; black belt.
ACCESSORIES: Versace sunglasses with colored lenses; Swiss watch;
perfect five o'clock shadow; keys to expensive foreign auto; tiny cell
phone; money clip; cigarettes; female.
PLUMAGE: Slick; gelled hair.

Female
EXTERIOR: Tight black dress.
MARKINGS: Heavily made up.
ACCESSORIES: Tiny cell phone; martini; cigarettes.

xisting in a near-constant state of bacchanalia, these Hipsters are
our most hedonistic, eclipsing other similarly debauched yet less
well-funded species in terms of sheer drunken revelry [*see*
Ravers]. Centered entirely upon the concept of flaunting one's wealth in
the gaudiest manner possible, ET have managed to construct an environment, termed the "club," perfectly tailored to their proclivity for excess. Though said terrain is recommended for observation, *admission is
often prohibitive.* Those not in possession of an unlimited social budget
or lacking female companionship of an appropriately noteworthy physical designation are advised that *attempting entrance may be a risk to
their own egos.*

EuroTrash are more materialistic than Men Who Lunch, more ostentatious than Socialites, consume more alcohol than Ex-Frats, yearn for
power more fervently than Alpha Females, etc. [*see* separate entries]. Due
to this phenomenon, certain prominent experts have chosen to focus primarily on this species, believing that they (i.e., EuroTrash) represent
something of the avant-garde in terms of Hipster evolution [e.g., M. Tom-
linson's *Broken Dreams and English*, B. Callaghan's *Velvet Ropeburn,* or
Dadlani's seminal, yet never completed, *Cocaine, Brazilian Wax and I*].

Label:

While many specimens who indulge in the EuroTrash lifestyle are indeed European [e.g., the young Portuguese population of Fall River, MA], the majority of these Hipsters do not, in fact, hail from the Continent. However, as inaccurate in terms of geography the name "Euro Trash" may be, its suggestion of disparagement is quite apt.* These Hipsters are, after all, almost universally reviled [*see* below]. Questions of actual origin aside, "EuroTrash" is accurate also in its summation of these Hipsters' general aesthetic; that is, they are European in that they strive to embody what they consider to be the height of European (read, in large part, Italian) fashion [e.g., Armani, Gucci, Ferragamo, et al.].

The species employs its own label on exceedingly rare occasions, and only then in a spirit of good-natured self-mockery. The term is often shortened to the somewhat more pleasant form "Euro," though most experts theorize that this crude amputation isn't fooling anyone.

Finances:

Much of the disdain leveled at this species is a direct result of their seemingly endless supply of cash money, coupled with the fact that these Hipsters have done little (if anything) to warrant such reward. The concept of earning money is practically as foreign to them as they are to us.

Many specimens live off a parentally provided allowance. In order to meet the high demands dictated by their social lives, this allowance is excessive; it is not unusual for certain Hipsters to receive in excess of $10,000 per week. Yes, per week. The origin of this money is the subject of great speculation; most is believed cultivated through corrupt foreign means, the details of which remain decidedly murky.

Power:

EuroTrash are fueled by a desire to manifest and exert power. Such behavior is a mainstay of the species' club-hopping activities, from entrance to eventual passing out. These Hipsters expend great energy (and money) cultivating relationships with choice nightspots [*see* Habitat, below].

*The term "EuroTrash" is believed to be American in origin.

While introductions are sometimes provided by other ex-pats, more often than not a good deal of personal "greasing" of club bouncers is necessary. Once said relationship has been successfully established, ET are able to wield their greatest power, an ability to instantaneously circumnavigate even the longest line of prospective club patrons [Figure 1]. This ability is so impressive that some experts suspect the very presence of a line exists solely to provide these Hipsters an obstacle to haughtily outmaneuver.

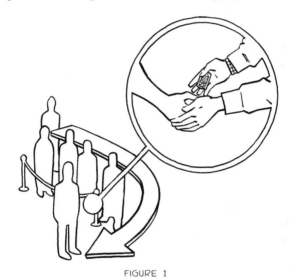

FIGURE 1

Such activity is mutually beneficial, as club owners profit by attracting a high-roller clientele and, once inside, the largesse continues unabated. Not wishing to mingle with the hoi polloi, ET purchase their own table, a desire communicated through a complex and instinctual pattern of bared teeth, wrinkled noses, and cocked ears. By occupying a table, the species tacitly agrees to consume alcohol "by the bottle," an arrangement which normally costs upward of $300 per.

Habitat:
Best observed at night, these Hipsters are indigenous to terrain normally considered unappealing by most experts due to high levels of

Techno Music and exorbitant entrance fees. The frugal observer may wish to simply linger alfresco, where EuroTrash may be glimpsed, albeit briefly, in the acts of entry or exit. Those willing to expend great patience may be rewarded with the sight of a specimen carefully parking his foreign sports car.

In Boston, MA:

ARMANI CAFÉ *(214 Newbury Street)*—"Dancing on tables" requires energy, and fortunately this fashion emporium/restaurant offers "fabulous" Italian sustenance perfect for "pre-club" dining. In addition to providing the expected "see or be seen" atmosphere, the staff is attentive (provided that you come equipped with sufficient "moulah") and the smoking section "reminds me of Rome."

In Los Angeles, CA:

THE CENTURY CLUB *(10131 Constellation Boulevard, Century City)*— Don't forget your "foreign nationalist parent's credit cards," because everything at this entertainment mega-complex, from the "valet" to the "shots," is wildly expensive. Party with "Lakers and bankers" or "drop a few hundred" on sushi upstairs before "groping girls" to "salsa" music. While not quite as upscale as it once was, the club's hip-hop cachet helps lend patrons "more street cred than anyone back in Buenos Aires."

In Miami Beach, FL:

OPIUM GARDEN *(136 Collins Avenue)*—Packed with the most attractive club-goers in "South Beach," this outdoor trance haven is "*the* place" to order a "$700 bottle of Cristal," "shatter a few tables," and try to "sneak into Janet Jackson's VIP party." Things can get "pretty wild," so don't be surprised if your "Lexus needs to be redetailed" after "puking in it" after leaving.

In New York, NY:

AU BAR *(41 East 58th Street)*—Locals say "I like is dance" at this Midtown institution noted for its "good experience of music" and "women and men looking hot all night." The doorman "can be real pain," though once inside "DJ play best music" and the bartenders pour the "greatest drinks for hot chicks and honeys." Even "Amir managed to score with girls," so don't miss this club if you're "loaded and wanting the sex."

RAVERS

CLUBKIDDUM OSTENTATIA

CANDY

BACKPACK

GOGGLES

GLOWSTICK

WATER

RAVERS

EXTERIOR: Garish, wide-legged pants (dark solid or vertical piping with vertical reflective stripe, side inserts, or patches) or overalls; multiple large pockets (for holding pills, bottled water, pacifiers, etc.); zip-up "hoodie" shirt or vest; one-strap shirt, halter top, mini- or slit skirt (female); T-shirt (male).

ACCESSORIES: Messenger bag; reflective belts and bracelets; glowsticks; bottled water; Discman; Ecstasy.

PLUMAGE: Brightly dyed (neon green, orange, pink), bleached, or jet black; affixed with small barrettes or rubber bands with round balls; messily gelled; glittery.

Peppy in the extreme, these Hipsters are noted for their pursuit of complete hedonism and exist in a near-constant state of frenzied partying. Though largely assumed to represent a 1990s youth phenomenon, the species actually finds its roots in the 1960s Hippie counterculture [see below and separate entry]. Over the last forty years, however, Ravers have managed to shed any serious political leanings and have devolved into a species wholly consumed by the practice of dancing, coupled with the ingestion of man-made psychoactive chemicals [esp. MDMA, see below].

Ravers are one of a few species to embrace their own label. They reject the concept of individuality and take great pains to assimilate into a herd. Their aggressively garish appearance serves scant tangible purpose, save for identification. *The species is strongly recommended for beginners venturing into the field.*

PLUR:

Once the approved and official acronym of Rave culture, PLUR [Peace Love Unity Respect] has recently fallen somewhat out of favor. However, the term [coined, according to Rave Legend, during a speech given by Frankie Bones, the Founding Father of American Raves, ca. 1990] still neatly illustrates the species' general disposition and world-view.* Ravers are inclined to live their lives according to the tenets represented by PLUR; that is, they are diligent in their efforts to appear über-sensitive and sincere. Even when mired in the worst of situations [e.g., bottled water delivery delayed, "Ecstasy" actually Bayer, glowstick on the fritz, etc.], these Hipsters cling to the misbegotten belief that "it's all good."

E[†]

These Hipsters depend completely upon a man-made chemical for survival. Methylenedioxymethamphetamine ($C_{11}H_{15}NO_2$, or MDMA), a compound referred to colloquially as Ecstasy, is to the Raver what alcohol is to the Ex-Frat [*see* entry], a veritable life source doubling as pleasure provider. Possessing both stimulant and hallucinogenic properties, this wonder drug supplies what are normally naturally occurring traits, such as personality, energy, and joy, to this simpleminded and otherwise dull species.

During the roughly five-hour period of Ecstasy-fueled exhilaration, these Hipsters remain happy, excited, and touchy-feely. Intensified by loud music, these effects result in prolonged episodes of feverish and trippy dancing, hugging, and mad grinning. Ravers under the influence also boast profound levels of empathy, even toward those undeserving. While in such a state, they are quite impossible to reason with, though intense flirtation is generally well received.

Natural Enemy:

In terms of the Hipster Kingdom, Ravers possess no serious natural enemy, though the mopeyness of Goths and the violence of Punks serve as points of divergence and are heavily frowned upon [*see* entries].

The species' real enemies are the Mass Media and Outsiders, both of whom threaten their survival through attempts to misrepresent or expose the scene. Ravers are consumed with the concept of misrepresen-

*Though grammatically foolish, PLUR is sometimes employed as an adjective. *When outside of Raver-specific terrain, such usage is discouraged.*

[†]In many circles, Ecstasy is referred to as "X," not "E," though this species tends to prefer the latter.

tation and are adamantly opposed to their lifestyle's classification as one of mere recreation, especially through depictions focusing on the negative aspects of teen drug abuse. Interestingly, these Hipsters believe that they are actually a part of something unique and revolutionary, despite substantial evidence suggesting a practically humanwide love of drugs and dancing.

Infighting:

Despite determined efforts to remain as fluffy and lovable as possible, a good deal of intraspecies animosity does exist. The majority of this bickering involves the term "Raver" and just who may label themselves as such. Certain specimens adopt Rave culture through the simple act of consumption; that is, through the purchase of Rave tickets, clothes, drugs, music, and etc. Though perhaps constituting a sizable majority, these cretins are derided for having severed ties to the underground movement once integral to the scene.

The term "Raver" itself has been rejected by militant, "true" practitioners [i.e., DJs, musicians, promoters, visual crews, and assorted underground participants] in favor of "Groover" or "Partykid." Likewise, "Raves" are referred to as "Parties," "Events," or "Gatherings."

Plumage; Accessories:

These Hipsters draw attention to themselves and to the fact that they have been successfully indoctrinated into a scene through each sartorial decision made. Ravers prefer that their hair and clothing be as bright, outrageous, and easily identifiable as possible. Rave Hair Kits are widely available on the Internet, and most come with detailed instructions for the less creative. Clothing is handled in a similar manner and may be ordered en masse. Largely eschewing tattoos, these Hipsters are fervent adherents to the practice of piercing, especially in easy-to-spot locations such as the face.

Certain accessories, however, are useful for purposes other than the celebration of marginality. Candy (esp. lollipops, blow pops, and gum) provides a helpful sugar rush for dancing and helps alleviate MDMA-induced teeth grinding. The ubiquitous pacifier is preposterous enough to be grouped among other useless Rave-related props [e.g., glowsticks, whistles, etc.] despite its ability to also alleviate dental friction.

Habitat:

Ravers are a nomadic species. Not native to any known natural environment, they must commandeer terrain of large acreage for their own purposes. Abandoned warehouses, secluded fields, and airplane hangars suffer high levels of Rave exploitation. Raves are often held at a location only once and sometimes under a cloak of secrecy. It is imperative, therefore, to establish some level of inside information prior to attempting field study.

In the Nevada Desert:
BURNING MAN *(Adjacent to large wooden male effigy)*—"Trippier" than "three hits of DMT," this celebration of creativity and "naked flesh" promotes peace, harmony, and "really bad art." Be sure to pack plenty of "dance drugs," as the "Hippies" and their "cannabis" can be a real "buzz kill." Whether stumbling about in a "Ketamine daze," organizing a "puppy pile," or just fretting over the possibility of a "speed willy," this communal festival is "pharmo-tastic."

In New York, NY:
MCDONALD'S *(25–27 Third Avenue)*—Order a "Number one, super-sized, with water" at this "happening" "chillout" spot where "adrenaline"-deficient locals flock to be "stared at" while refueling after a rough night of "glowsticking." The fluorescent lighting scheme is "really ambient," while the "nuggets" make some feel "luvdup." Regulars "rave" "the Shamrock Shake is kicking!"

In Portland, OR:

ABANDONED WAREHOUSE *(address TBA)*—Rumored to be "totally mental," even "plassies" are determined to discern the precise location of this event, though some complain, "the tipline is disconnected!" Those "in the know" got the details when "the flyer dropped last week" and are so "psyched" that even "tranx" and "holotropic breathing" won't curtail their adventures in the "feely feely room."

In Southern California:

CAMP TRIPPY *(details at* www.camptrippy.com*)*—This eighteen-hour campout/"psychoactive mindfreak" will be more than worth the half-hour "trip" from LA, if only for the "techno" marshmallow roasting. "Security" might be "bogus," so most visitors suggest "stacking" on the drive down or seeking out "snarlers" inside. The "optical light show" and "bottled water vendors" almost make up for having to "shit in the woods."

The *Liberalia* Family

THREE SPECIES:

1. ACADEMICS (LARVAL)

2. ACTIVISTS (LEFTIST)

3. HIPPIES

Still sunning themselves in the afterglow of the 1960s, the following species have experienced something of a steady decline in the years subsequent to their fleeting heydays. While energy and determination have remained steady, almost all relevancy has significantly waned. Of the three, Academics are perhaps the least conspicuous, limiting their exploits, as they do, to long, digressive lecturing or the occasional snide commentary.

ACADEMICS (LARVAL)*

SHABBYLIUM ERUDITA

OVERBITE

HUNCHED

EYEBROWS COCKED
CONDESCENDINGLY

HUNCHED

HAND-ME-DOWN

THESIS

*Though certainly not Hip by most standards, the species' peculiarly insular mores and rampant exclusivity allow them to sneak in through a broad definition.

Male
EXTERIOR: Tweed blazer; sweater vest; corduroy slacks; denim jeans.

Female
EXTERIOR: Mismatched patterns, frayed or faded fabric.

Both Sexes
PLUMAGE: Tousled, unkempt hair.
ACCESSORIES: Satchel, book bag, or knapsack; dissertation; hot tea in mug.
VOICE: Nasal song; sniffling.

A cademics are similar to Internet Geeks [*see* entry] in that they are unable to appreciate or even recognize the larger social landscape. While seemingly quite intelligent, certain observers have noted the species' penchant for drearily uninteresting topics [e.g., Philip Pauly's *Fighting the Hessian Fly: American and British Responses to Insect Invasion, 1776–1789* or Susan Klepp's *Colds, Worms, and Hysteria: Menstrual Regulation in Eighteenth-Century America*], thus calling into question the validity of their presumed superiority. Whether or not these Hipsters do indeed possess some intrinsic brilliance, their shocking inability to realize tangible, real-world achievement hinders their movement when outside of academic terrain. *In such environments, Academics may appear dim-witted and slow-moving; observation from extremely close proximity may prove possible.*

Physical Traits:
Of supreme interest to most observers is the female's apparent Post-Undergrad Fashion Gap. The desultory and out-of-date sartorial habits of this creature are regarded not as the result of a lifelong inability to accessorize, but as a complete termination of the practice upon cessation of undergraduate study. Interestingly, such habits do not lend a hip

"retro" appearance. As their clothing actually dates from the period, and is not an expensively purchased approximation of any given era, their articles often exhibit a certain degree of unsightly decay.

Males generally do not suffer from the same abhorrent level of dress as does the female. In fact, many such specimens actually exhibit a strangely suave, if geeky, overall appearance.

Both sexes are normally quite pale, owing to their rarely venturing out-of-doors other than to pace briskly across university courtyards. The species exhibits little muscle tone, due to disdain for most physical activity (save, perhaps, occasional emotionally detached coitus). Academics are particularly prone to reading-related injury [e.g., paper cuts, Lecturer's Neck, etc.].

The species also exhibits a somewhat maniacal passion for hot tea, preferably British in blend. This insatiable habit results not only in an overly caffeinated detachment but in aggressively bad breath as well. *Maintain a reasonable distance.*

Metamorphosis:
Larval Academics experience two stages of development: pre- and post-Ph.D. The former take the form of Teaching Assistants (TAs) or Teaching Fellows (TFs). These specimens inhabit the lowest position of the academic totem pole and reside one step above mere undergrads. Usually graduate students, they possess the rare ability to enchant their charges despite possession of a near-absolute dork countenance. Many undergrads, in fact, have been known to receive passing grades based more on their ability to flirt than academic prowess.

The latter stage, while constituting a great step out from the swamps of pre-Ph.D. marginalization, enjoys a decidedly tenuous foothold in the world of academia. Adjunct, Assistant, or Associate Professors at best, these Hipsters are required to actually teach students, as opposed to their superiors' [e.g., Professors, Distinguished Professors, Professors Emeritus] ability to wile away their days in office-bound seclusion, sitting on committees or writing grant proposals and articles. Such older specimens will deign to instruct perhaps one class per semester, usually in the interest of padding the syllabus with texts of their own authorship.

Mating Rituals:

Male Academics prefer impressionable coeds as mates. Usually conducted during a period referred to as "office hours," their mating dance involves a delicate balance of extra credit, affected brilliance, large words, public radio, feigned altruism, and red ink. Most males pursue somewhat flighty, buxom, flaxen-haired young women with marginal grades and a need for guidance.

Relatively little is known of the female's sexual proclivities, except that when officially engaged, she exhibits a tendency to hyphenate her surname with that of her husband.

Raison d'être:

Academics condescend on a near–Judeo-Christian Godlike level. They experience no thrill like the rush of hearing their own voices. This condescension is aimed at targets both intra- and interspecies, as they know no creature to whom they feel inferior. In general, however, Academics who have received Ph.D.'s from prominent universities [e.g., Princeton; Harvard] outrank those who have attended, shall we say, lesser institutions [e.g., Ocean County College; Boston University]. Likewise, condescension may be derived by publication in prominent, well-respected journals [e.g., *Clinical Child Psychology and Psychiatry*], as opposed to any old rag [e.g., *British Journal of Ethnomusicology*]. *Unless one is being graded, much of what they say may be ignored.*

Habitat:

These Hipsters spend the vast majority of their lives on campus and, obviously, university grounds are ideal terrain for observation. Specifically, Academics seem to prefer such environs as offices, courtyards, and affiliated "centers" (terrain underwritten by the given university and which, while theoretically devoted to the promotion of a specific discipline, serves mainly to pad the résumés of those involved). When off campus, these Hipsters tread only upon terrain of a decidedly sophisticated sort, such as cafés, bookshops, and libraries.

In Berkeley, CA:

CODY'S BOOKS *(2454 Telegraph Avenue)*—If you're in the mood for love, "Barry Richard Burg's *Sodomy and the Pirate Tradition: English Sea Rovers in the Seventeenth Century Caribbean*," or just "Pierre Bourdieu's *Distinction: A Social Critique of the Judgment of Taste*," this legendary shop, while perhaps not as "revolutionary" as in the past, is still "quite more than adequate." From the "breadth" of its "periodicals" to its out-of-print, hard-to-find specialties, most "discerning" customers regard this institution as "closer, ultimately, to a true friend than any human I've thus far encountered."

In Cambridge, MA:

MIRACLE OF SCIENCE BAR & GRILL *(321 Massachusetts Avenue)*—"According to Einstein," beer goes "relatively" well with "quantitative" female "analysis" and "dissections" of the "comparative athletic norms" "inherent to" "any given" Beantown sporting club. The atmosphere is so comfortable, many regulars find themselves seated "longer than Stephen Hawking."

In New York, NY:

HUNGARIAN PASTRY SHOP *(1030 Amsterdam Avenue bet. 111th Street and Cathedral Parkway)*—For old-fashioned, traditional treats and available light that's "dimmer than an undergrad's thesis statement," Columbia "smartrons" flock to this "fin de siècle" campus coffee shop that provides a perfect respite from "writing grant proposals" or "humoring the dean's wife at that luncheon."

LABYRINTH BOOKS *(536 West 112th Street)*—Have your research assistant "keep an eye on the phones" and head over to this "literate" bargain book emporium noted for having "eight copies of my dissertation" and sale prices "perfectly suited to my seventeenth-century itinerant laborer's salary." Though the sometimes "provincial" nature of the staff may hinder your search for "Tawney's *Religion and the Rise of Capitalism*," regulars invoke "cultural relativism" to account for their "startling incompetence."

ACTIVISTS (LEFTIST)*

IDEALISTICA GAUCHE

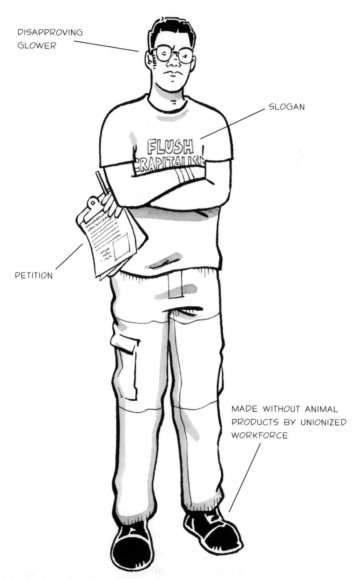

DISAPPROVING
GLOWER

SLOGAN

PETITION

MADE WITHOUT ANIMAL
PRODUCTS BY UNIONIZED
WORKFORCE

FLUSH
CRAPITALISM

*Activists do exist on the political Right. However, their often fanatical adherence to Christian doctrine and fondness for nonurban, largely unenlightened terrain [e.g., the Bible Belt] place them outside the categorization of Hip.

ACTIVISTS

EXTERIOR: Cargo pants; military-style boots; T-shirt.
ACCESSORIES: Thick "pleather" bracelets; eyeglasses.
PLUMAGE: Sometimes bandanna-obscured hair.
VOICE: Loud, piercing, and guttural.

The most illogical and hysterical of all Hipsters, Activists *should be approached with extreme trepidation*, as they will strike at the slightest suggestion of either ignorance or opposition. The species is incredibly confrontational; though at times capable of violence [*see* below], the majority of their aggressive acts are limited to regurgitated sermonizing or loud chanting arranged in sophomoric rhyme schemes.

Despite possessing a low capacity for cognitive activity and an inability to process complex, rational ideas, these Hipsters exhibit a rare ability to store vast quantities of raw data. Activists soak up and retain reams of statistical information in order to lend some semblance of evidentiary substance to their largely theoretical arguments. By regurgitating said data en masse, the species is able to successfully engender feelings of inadequacy in even their most learned adversaries.

Origin of the Species:
Comprised largely of the white and privileged, the species propagates itself on collegiate terrain, where most specimens are indoctrinated according to the principles of the local Activist Club [viz., an attitudinal swing to the Left, plus acceptance of the fact that things disapproved of, such as fast food or leather, are not only unfortunate, but actually Evil]. Once brainwashed, these Hipsters enjoy the status of minor (and irritating) campus celebrities. At this early stage of growth, Activists participate in the deriding and protesting of such important and prevalent abominations as Non-Vegan Food Courts, Columbus Day Observance,

and Athletic Footwear Purchasing. Many excel at low-tech flyer dissemination, creative sticker arrangement, and liberal arts studying.

Theorizing:

Most arguments made by these Hipsters sound nice enough on paper, but prove utterly ridiculous when applied to the real world. Experts point to the Activist's pet cause, Anti-Capitalism/Globalization, as a succinct example of this practical application gap. Entire herds have been known to descend upon urban centers in order to parade about in garish homemade costumes, taunt police officers, listen to U2, spit at Starbucks' windows, and display the latest in handwritten signage [Figure 1]. On such occasions, nary a thoughtful alternative is heard proposed, as Activists instinctively balk at presenting any reasonable alternative (with the possible exception of theoretically good ideas, such as socialism, Marxism, communism, et al.).

FIGURE 1

Rationalization:

Activists are able to rationalize the merits of any and all activity undertaken personally, while simultaneously condemning similar behavior on the part of their enemies.* The most striking example of this instinctual fallacy may be found in the species' long and much-publicized Peace prerogative. Antiwar and antiviolence, Activists often assume a decidedly militaristic approach in terms of both fashion and behavior.

Furthermore, they are pro-violence when such tactics serve their purposes and rationalize that such endeavors are warranted when undertaken in the service of approved causes. For example, Activists excel at acts of vandalism [e.g., tossing fake blood on women draped in fur, spray-painting the slogan "We Won" on police cruisers post-riot, shattering the windows of a Warner Bros. store etc.], and even go so far as to regard such activity as art or a form of expression.

Multitasking:

Activists are rarely required to suffer any personal indignity before pledging their allegiance to a cause; that is, for example, few Slave Reparations Activists have actually been slaves. Moreover, these Hipsters are able to simultaneously support a large number of completely disconnected, even dissimilar issues [e.g., gay rights, AIDS activism, anti–racial profiling, environmentalism, anti–death penalty, pro welfare, animal rights, et al.].

Most specimens do, however, align themselves most fervently with one specific cause, of which some are admirable (environmentalism), abhorrent (Free Mumia), or so obvious as to seem almost not worth the effort or bumper stickers (antirape). Given the species' well-documented lack of originality, it is fortunate that many great minds have devoted themselves to the effort of swaying these largely uninformed Hipsters [e.g., Beastie Boys, Rage Against The Machine, Janeane Garofalo, etc.].

Habitat:

Regardless of terrain, it is important to keep in mind that these Hipsters rarely refrain from pontification, even in the interest of mutually

*Perhaps the most preposterous example of the species' mentality may be found in the anti-commercial rag *Adbusters*' propensity to advertise and sell products within its pages, such as an outrageously overpriced ($35!) fifteen-minute VHS anthology of social marketing campaigns [offered, incidentally, in an issue which simultaneously expounded upon the virtues of something called "Buy Nothing Day," Autumn 1997].

enjoyable lunch conversation. As a result, *personal contact should be entered into strictly at the risk of the observer.*

In Kent, OH:

THE STUDENT CENTER, KENT STATE UNIVERSITY *(intersection of Risman Drive and Summit Street)*—"Start a committee" or "two" at this hotbed of "Third World advocacy" and "dated social import." While regulars rave that "denouncing sweatshops" is a "great way to meet people," faculty members simply "humor" the "idealistic drivel" and "largely uninformed" opinions of undergraduate "liberal arts majors."

In New York, NY:

NIKETOWN *(5 East 57th Street)*—"Blockade the front doors" and suffer "police brutality" at this Midtown complex noted for its "exploitative" "slave labor," violation of "Vietnamese labor law," and "highly fashionable" athletic wear. "International Anti-Nike Day" is a perfect occasion for "holding Phillip Knight accountable," "lambasting Michael Jordan," or "organizing" your next "letter-writing campaign."

In Seattle, WA:

STARBUCKS COFFEE *(various locations)*—Gather to "demand the sale of Free Trade coffee!" at this comfortable respite that's "almost more insidious than the Gap." Perfectly suited for "environmentalists" in need of a "convenient target," these cafés are "reviled" for their practice of "single-handedly crippling small farmers" and "unconscionably" refusing to provide "hormone-free cream for my latte." That neither claim is "factually correct" does little to influence the opinion that "generally, corporations are fundamentally flawed and built on exploiting the people."

In Washington, D.C.:

STATE OF THE UNION *(1357 U Street NW)*—"Think globally, drink locally" while lamenting the "desperate cynicism of postmodern decadence" or fondly "remembering Sacco and Vanzetti" over a bottle of "red" at this popular Soviet-themed dance and Happy Hour joint conveniently located "literally within spitting distance" of American democracy. Even "Freedom for Palestine" makes more sense after a few "$1 beers."

HIPPIES

PEACENIKA TRIPPYUM

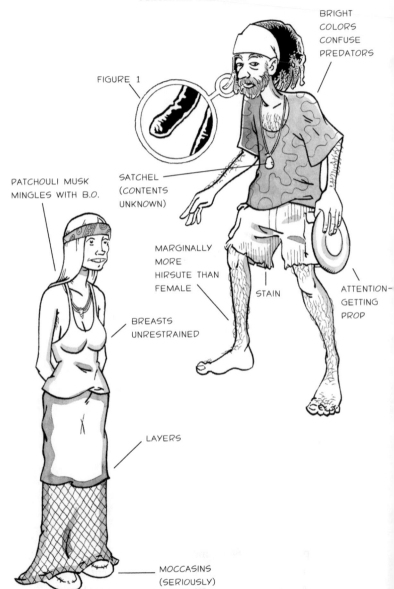

BRIGHT COLORS CONFUSE PREDATORS

FIGURE 1

SATCHEL (CONTENTS UNKNOWN)

PATCHOULI MUSK MINGLES WITH B.O.

MARGINALLY MORE HIRSUTE THAN FEMALE

STAIN

BREASTS UNRESTRAINED

ATTENTION-GETTING PROP

LAYERS

MOCCASINS (SERIOUSLY)

As members of the only species savvy enough to actually incorporate the word "hip" into its very name, these Hipsters have assured their classification despite an utter lack of authenticity. With the death of Jerry Garcia in 1995 and the resulting dissolution of the Grateful Dead, Hippies lost not only their driving center but also their final tangible link to the present. These Hipsters are the only species to function in the manner of a tribute band. The depth and social relevance of an earlier generation [e.g., Vietnam, Civil Rights, etc.] has been replaced by little more than disaffected laziness and lame political rallying [e.g., legalizing marijuana]. The species has evolved somewhat since the 1960s, but in a largely insignificant manner [i.e., fewer tie-dyed T-shirts, more Ben & Jerry's flavors].

Hippies exhibit a shocking lack of self-awareness and seem unable to recognize the irony of their own appearance; though once the gold standard of youth counterculture, they currently exhibit the dress, politics, outlook, lingo, tastes, and general goofiness of their parents' generation, the current Establishment.

Grooming:

This hirsute species is among our most slovenly. They regard their lack of cleanliness as a sophisticated piece of anti-establishment, noncorporate commentary. As a result of this aversion to bathing, many Hippies possess a singularly offputting odor. *A reasonable distance is normally recommended, though the species is perfectly suited for identification by the blind.* In residential terrain, Hippies are regularly excluded from furniture-based comfort and are instead relegated to the floor in efforts to limit laundering and fumigation expense. Such precautionary measures are met with the species' tiresome rallying cry "the body is beautiful."

The greatest triumph of their filthiness is the dreadlock hairstyle [Figure 1]. The abominable coif is sometimes made further ridiculous by the additions of hair wraps (friendship bracelets for the head), Indian beads, or small shells.

Mind Alteration:
Owing to an underdeveloped social cortex, these Hipsters rely heavily on illicit pharmaceuticals for purposes of personality and recreation. Marijuana is the undisputed king of Hippie drugs [e.g., Cheech and Chong], its distinctive green leaf the subject of many VW Bus retrospective paint jobs. Calls to legalize the drug are a mainstay of Hippie politics and the basis both for magazine production [e.g., *High Times*] and urban park gatherings [e.g., Boston's "Hemp Fest"].

In addition to the gentle high provided by marijuana, the species has been known to expand its consciousness through the use of hallucinogenic (or "psychedelic") drugs, most notably LSD (acid).* Also popular, if less potent, are environmentally friendly "Shrooms." Few spectacles provide more amusement than the sight of Hippies on bad "trips" [e.g., the brown acid at Woodstock]. However, one should *exercise caution in such terrain, as they like to be held. Demur.* The species' fondness for substance-enhanced activity has spawned several cottage industries, such as laser light show development and hackey sack production.

Raison d'être:
Without the incessant touring of the Grateful Dead, experts speculate that the species would have run its course decades ago, in a manner

*Today, many specimens have abandoned acid in favor of the trendy interspecies' favorite Ecstasy.

similar to most epoch-specific Hipsters [e.g., Flappers, Greasers, Dandies, Beats, Black Militants, etc.]. Many specimens followed the band from city to city in a great and malodorous caravan. The parking lot outside each venue doubled as a temporary commune in which Hippies camped, did drugs, had sex, braided things, eschewed shaving, played with devil sticks [Figure 2], formed friendships, rallied for leftist/progressive causes, formed drum circles, and displayed their unmatched sympathy for animals by tying hemp-collared Labradors to truck bumpers during the actual concert. Sadly, herds of this size have been all but decimated and no longer roam free in nature.

FIGURE 2

Having seen the Dead is a rigid requirement for full-fledged Hippie indoctrination. Certain specimens were even rumored to have put off college in order to follow the band. Hipsters of post–Jerry Garcia (A.G.) vintage are doubly anachronistic, as they are essentially a tribute to an already tributary species. *If questioned on the subject of Dead viewing, answer in the affirmative and be prepared to offer, upon request, dates, cities, and intimate knowledge of the given set list (including medleys).*

Habitat:
Hippies are indigenous to terrain featuring a certain natural element. Despite the advent of such luxuries as running water, heat, and refrig-

eration, these Hipsters seem to actually enjoy spending time outdoors. In addition to the species' proclivity to undertake strange excursions known as "camping" or "hiking," these Hipsters are drawn to environments that lend an aspect of Mother Earth to their everyday routines, be it in the form of mountains, forests, valleys, or streams.

In Boulder, CO:

PENNY LANE COFFEE HOUSE *(1795 Pearl Street)*—"Patchouli"-soaked "Granolas" flock to this charming café, where the caffeine rush is "psychedelic." While some prefer to sit alone and "take it easy" with their "mantra," most "brothers and sisters" congregate to "compare body odor" or discuss "devil stick technique." Whether cooling down after a tough round of "hackey sack" or prepping for a long night of "corduroy slack alteration," this local fave is a real "turn-on."

In Burlington, VT:

NECTAR'S *(188 Main Street)*—This "righteous" bar and music "establishment," best known for giving "Phish" their start, is a favorite "hang" of local "teenyboppers" and "strung-out" homeless "folks." "Primo" cafeteria-style food perfectly complements any drink; some say the homemade onion rings are "right on" and "even better than orange sunshine." Due to its late-night "scene," you won't need to "split" until 2:00 A.M.

In Eugene, OR:

OUT OF THE FOG *(450 Willamette Street)*—"Be here now!" rave regulars who "keep the faith" at this popular café and hangout. The coffee is "hip," so get "behind it." Feel free to just relax and "do your own thing"; "don't be so uptight, man." Some feel the caffeine is "a bummer," but others advise "if it feels good, do it." Grab a "bongo" and indulge in some "old-fashioned drum circling" or just sit back and "extol the benefits of reforestation."

In Madison, WI:

SUNSHINE DAYDREAM *(434 State Street)*—For some "mellow" and marijuana-fueled "good times," this head shop filled with "trippy" people and "positive vibes" is definitely "where it's at." If "the Man" wanders in, tell him "it's just tobacco," since drawing "the heat" is "more of a buzz kill than Altamont." Before you "split," locals recommend "pouring a little out for Jerry."

The *Ovum* Family

SIX SPECIES:

1. BUTCH / FEMME

2. ELIZABETH STREET SHOP GIRLS

3. MODELS

4. PERFORMANCE POETS

5. URBAN MOMS

6. VIDEO HOS

ALSO DISCUSSED:

SOCIALITES

The Hipster Kingdom is often male-dominated. For reasons not fully understood, many female specimens exhibit something of a passive disposition, so much so that deviations from this norm are often accorded fawning appreciation and lent a significance possibly not in keeping with their actual worth [e.g., The Donnas]. However, the following species are noteworthy for featuring a dominant female. As such, males are considered mere window dressing and observation should be kept to a minimal, fleeting level at best.

BUTCH/FEMME

MASCULINA APPROXIMUM / SAPPHICCUM LIPSTICKA

TATTOOS

FLANNEL

BOYISHLY CUTE

STURDY

BUTCH

EXTERIOR: Mullet or buzz haircut; wife-beater undershirt; cargo shorts; denim; flannel.
ACCESSORIES: Leather wrist band; wallet chain.
MARKINGS: Mixed; often female-themed.
VOICE: Affected baritone.

FEMME

EXTERIOR: Varies greatly. Often either vampy (red lips; boobs) or slightly rough around the edges, yet cute (conservative piercings; shorn hair).

Though technically two separate species, these Hipsters' proclivity for cohabitation, coupled with their practically identical philosophies and politics, warrants the traditional act of grouping for purposes of description, as well as identification.

On officially established Lesbian terrain, most specimens skew toward Butch, as they represent, in many ways, the face of contemporary, empowered Lesbianism. *For males venturing into the field, this can prove quite disappointing.* Except for the somewhat rarer Transgenders, these Hipsters display the most obvious renunciation of traditional femininity among *Ovum* species, preferring a decidedly masculine appearance. It is they who, normally, wear the strap-on. Many Butches also have been observed picking up checks, driving motorcycles, and wearing wife-beaters. They are strong, powerful, and in charge of all situations. *Approach with caution. They can and will kick your ass as a point of pride. Fighting back is discouraged as, technically, they're girls.*

Femmes, on the other hand, while equally as vocal in their declarations of "pussy power" (through such preferred means as Spoken Word, web sites, amateurish video production, and T-shirt design), retain many of the delightful characteristics for which females are often held in high esteem. This is not to suggest, however, that these Hipsters adhere completely to traditional modes of feminine appeal [e.g., blond-haired midwestern cheerleaders]. On the contrary, Femmes are often slightly rough around the edges, fond of severely chopped hair and facial piercings. Still, most specimens are quite adorable and, if only by contrast, wildly desirable. *While observation is usually tolerated, approach is actively discouraged.*

Sisterhood:

Both species latch on to and adore any public figure confirmed as Lesbian or even Lesbian-friendly [e.g., Melissa Etheridge, k.d. lang, Kathleen Hanna, Ellen DeGeneres, Madonna, Sandra Bernhard, Indigo Girls, Margaret Cho, et al.]. Few to no artistic standards need be met for acceptance to this pantheon, aside from a desire to engage in (or at least a palpable endorsement of) sexual activity with other girls.

Interestingly, this spell can occasionally be broken, as best illustrated by the case of singer Ani DiFranco. Long enamoured for her patently grating mix of sapphic folk music ("She Says") and punk rock aesthetics (the DIY ethics behind her Righteous Babe Records), the community reacted to the singer's 1998 wedding (to her sound guy, no less) with predictable displays of shocked betrayal.

Terminology:

While Lesbians-at-large are sometimes referred to as "Dykes" by certain less-sophisticated species [*see* Ex-Frats], these Hipsters have largely come to adopt the term as their own, even referring to larval specimens as "Baby Dykes." Similar to the "nigga" phenomenon, "dyke" can be safely uttered only by these Hipsters themselves. *Do not refer to them by this term within earshot.* The term "Butch" is similarly not recommended for casual use [*see* the 1996 Boston University Women's Softball Team versus one Mike Miller].

In a related matter, the word "queer" has also gained a large degree of acceptance, both in the Gay and Lesbian communities.

Politics:

These Hipsters are among our most political, specializing in hard-core, at times militant, feminism. Though schooled in the history of mainstream feminism, the species consider most platforms to be insufficiently radical.

Pride is central to the species' political positions. More often than not, their activism is aimed at gaining general acceptance rather than achieving any specific victory; the removal of societal stereotypes is the ultimate goal. Besides the time-honored political juggernaut that is parading, these Hipsters often express their agenda through artistic means. Specializing in poetry, the species employ said form as a means to express their specific brand of feminism and sexuality. Certain exceptionally disenfranchised specimens find the written word lacking strength and prefer instead the dreaded Spoken Word variety [*see* Performance Poets]. *Though good terrain for observation, sitting through such performances is not generally recommended.*

Habitat:

While these Hipsters may be spotted in virtually all terrain, certain reservations have been designated primarily for their habitation. Issues of timidity aside, non-*Ovum* observers are generally permitted to tread upon said terrain. However, certain environments will require some testament of homosexuality before entrance is allowed. *Answer, proudly, in the affirmative.* Female accompaniment is also recommended.

Their preferred terrain differs little from most bar or club settings. However, visitors should steel themselves to the screening of a seemingly endless loop of Lesbian-specific soft porn, particularly WNBA basketball games and the prepubescent exercise video *Teen Steam.*

In Los Angeles, CA:

PALMS *(8572 Santa Monica Boulevard)*—Every night is "Girls Night" at this no-frills (or "dicks") dance club, where Wednesdays feature $1 beers and "that girl on the patio looks sort of like Anne Heche." The theme nights are a "progressive" and "fun" concept, though their "labels" make some regulars uncomfortable. Still, the locale is perfect for "renouncing your femininity."

In New York, NY:

MEOW MIX *(269 East Houston Street)*—Like a "frat party for girls," this Lower East Side Lesbian mainstay features "beer," "strippers," and "practically male bouncers." Debate philosophical issues ("Would you have sex with the fifteen-year-old Alyssa Milano?"), lust after the "outrageously hot" barmaid, "compare breasts," or otherwise "objectify women from a female point of view." Be forewarned, due to the Great Lesbian Drought of '02, water actually costs "a dollar per glass."

REMOTE ["CLIT CLUB"] *(327 Bowery)*—Avoid the "phallic" video cam intrusions at this "bi"-level high-tech cyber lounge and head down to the basement for some "good old-fashioned homosexuality." Whether "flirting with girls" or "taking a boy home for fun," this dance party is "as stimulating as its name suggests." Males looking for "cheap thrills" are advised to "act gay" at the door.

In San Francisco, CA:

LEXINGTON CLUB *(3464 19th Street)*—A dive bar for "wimmin," "Dykes" of all kinds "come out" to shoot pool, "butch it up," or enjoy some casual, "non-penetrating" conversation in a relaxed atmosphere free from "breeders." While some older "Lesbos" have trouble "processing" the attitudes of "barely legal" "babies," most visitors manage to "come" back "multiple times."

ELIZABETH STREET SHOP GIRLS

FASHIONISTICA AUTEURUX

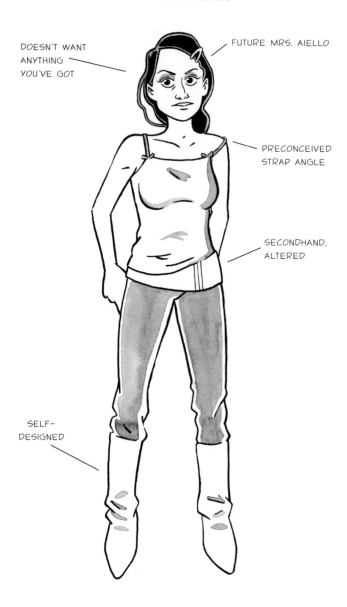

DOESN'T WANT ANYTHING YOU'VE GOT

FUTURE MRS. AIELLO

PRECONCEIVED STRAP ANGLE

SECONDHAND, ALTERED

SELF-DESIGNED

ELIZABETH STREET SHOP GIRLS

EXTERIOR: Denim jeans (7 Jeans; Katayone Adeli; Paper Denim & Cloth); Marc by Marc Jacobs; Sigerson Morrison boots; Sergio Rossi shoes; up-and-coming designer wear.
ACCESSORIES: Louis Vuitton logo bag (possibly purchased second-hand).

Though indigenous to a relatively minuscule and esoteric habitat, Elizabeth Street Shop Girls are so highly regarded by certain Hipsterati that their pursuit is not only recommended, but may reward the seasoned observer with particularly satisfying results. *They are enchanting. Allow ample time for observation and lingering.*

Origin of the Species; Migration:

Nestled between SoHo's shopping mall and the Lower East Side's bohemian grit, Elizabeth Street (and, by extension, its Hipsters) is a blend of its neighbors' better traits: high fashion (SoHo) and downtown artistic integrity (L.E.S.).

The ES Shop Girl is not only native to this terrain but solely responsible for its existence. Chafing under SoHo's escalating rents, these Hipsters migrated several blocks east, transforming an otherwise nondescript area into a charming village of boutiques and cafes.* Principally up-and-coming designers with European (read French) leanings, ES Shop Girls back up their bohemian ideals by exhibiting a legitimate talent for frock and tog design. Thus, the species distinguishes itself from packs of artistically lesser specimens, who self-promote, over drinks, while creating incoherent drivel [e.g., Boston University's film school, class of 1997].

---

*Ironically, the area has become so desirable that many Elizabeth Street Shop Girls can no longer afford to live there. These specimens have been forced to migrate farther afield, often to the East Village.

Reverse Slumming:

While approximating the appearance and trappings of wealth, most members of this species are in fact anything but well-to-do. The illusion of wealth is paramount. Except for actual shop owners and designers, most occupy low-level positions at fashion institutions [e.g., *Harper's Bazaar*, *Vogue*], pulling down measly salaries in the $30K range. They achieve and maintain their high level of style through habitual exploitation of industry perks, such as clothing "out of the closet," that is, left over from magazine shoots or reviews.

Furthermore, these Hipsters spend considerable time hanging out in each others' shops, spending little money throughout the course of any given day. Theirs is an illusion of cash-fueled leisure, an idle class for the creative.

Raison d'être:

ES Shop Girls pride themselves on the creation of a signature look. The species frowns upon the practice of draping oneself in any particular off-the-rack designer duds, regardless of how hip, stylish, or "in" said duds may be [e.g., Prada]. Such activity is thought contemptible due to the ease with which it is accomplished, as well as the lack of imagination required by such.

These Hipsters will wear designer "pieces," but usually only one at a time and mixed liberally with vintage articles or clothing of their own design. Accessories further enhance the spectacle; the species is rarely spotted in the field without an adorable, perfect purse or sunglasses [e.g., Chloé, Marc Jacobs]. Strangely, ES Shop Girls will occasionally don their sunglasses only *after* entering a café. Observation in such terrain is highly recommended and, in fact, quite desired.

Specimens not blessed with perfectly sleek physiques must maintain their appearance through continual upkeep. Of course, Elizabeth Street Shop Girls indulge only in the trendiest, most fashionable methods possible. As fish once climbed out of the sea and sprouted legs, this species recently melded its formerly preferred exercise techniques (yoga and Pilates) into an evolutionarily superior hybrid termed "yogalates." Survival of the fittest, indeed.

Predators:

Elizabeth Street Shop Girls live in constant fear of being overrun or infiltrated by their natural enemies, the Tourist (*Suburbum Philistina*). As their habitat continues to receive acclaim, the species has grown more weary and fearful of intruders. Tourists have been documented plundering the ES Shop Girls' natural resources, descending upon their fragile ecosystem with hefty bank accounts, wide hips, and rave notices from the latest issue of *W*. Poseurs, those yearning to fit in and willing to upgrade their entire wardrobe with one stroll through the neighborhood, often find themselves confronted with the species' lone defense mechanism: snootily detached sales service.

Vestigial Appendages:

Male specimens do occur in nature. Though quiet, cool, and fashionable, they are mere hangers-on and of note mainly for their enviable ability to coexist with ES Shop Girls.

Little is known of these elusive creatures other than their apparent lack of day jobs and penchant for driving caps. They excel, also, at drinking coffee and leaning suggestively in doorways.

Habitat:

Elizabeth Street Shop Girls (and hangers-on) are defined mostly by the geographical circumstances of their existence. Thus, observing these Hipsters is quite easy accomplished, as they stick mainly to their own terrain. Any number of local cafés and restaurants provide adequate vantage points for study as do, obviously, the shops themselves. Daytime observation is recommended.

In New York, NY:

CAFÉ GITANE *(242 Mott Street)*—"Francophiles" rejoice; this "European" "style" café is ideal for "lingering" over any number of "*délicieux*" items from "*un petit menu*" while "reflecting upon my favorite fabrics." Though "smoking" is now legally "gauche," rest assured that "cheek kissing" and "snobbery" are still encouraged. Don't forget to "sample" the couscous, which regulars claim "inspired my new line of swimwear."

CALYPSO *(280 Mott Street)*—Get reacquainted with your "inner girly girl" at this NoLita shop where "black" is definitely "so over" and "those Caribbean pants look like a freshman project at FIT." Given the "cheery," "bright" nature of the clothing, some find it surprising that the "failed models" behind the counter remain "so dour." For those attending an "urban luau" or just enjoying "a quiet night at home with my boyfriend and his parrot," locals recommend a "sarong" or "frilly" "tank top."

MAYLE *(252 Elizabeth Street)*—As "petite" as its customers, this "unassuming" "signless" storefront features "off-the-shoulder" blouses, "minor celebrity" customers, and "this stunning chemise I wish would go on sale." The "shop girls" offer "supportive, yet discreet" assistance to both "statuesque" locals and "that garish couple" visiting from "Orlando."

SIGERSON MORRISON *(28 Prince Street)*—Abandon "Nine West" for this "subtle" shop with "clean lines" and sales help with "attitude" right out of a "Steve Madden" ad. Even the prices are "sexy"; you won't have to "buckle" down too much to afford a pair of "chic" "flip-flops." Devoted regulars rave, "these black boots are as gorgeous as they are ubiquitous."

MODELS

PHYSICALLUM PERFECTA

WELL-DESERVED
VANITY

LEATHER

INTELLECTUAL
PEER

VACANT
STARE

POUT

6% BODY
FAT

POINTY
SHOES

MODELS

EXTERIOR: Designer, often willowy clothing (specifics vary greatly); altered according to trend and professional allegiance.
ACCESSORIES: Sunglasses; bags; small canine; Evian bottled water.
NESTING: As career wanes.

Noted as much for lack of depth as physical perfection, no logical rationale has been posited for the existence of such unaccountably alluring specimens (much to the chagrin of less-attractive siblings). Despite their often pedestrian origins, these Hipsters rarely deign to associate with the physically mundane (young comedic authors included).

The physicality upon which their success is based relegates the species to a relatively short life span. As they approach the advanced age of thirty, most Models are wisely encouraged either to settle down with an appropriate mate [i.e., Financiers, Film Directors, Restaurateurs, etc.], give birth to a tycoon's offspring (and prove paternity), or transform themselves into some bastardized version of their younger selves [e.g., SpokesModel, Infomercial Host, Tireless Crusader for Animal Rights, etc.].*

Interestingly, "The Rule of High School Inversion" provides for the fact that many members of this species were regarded as "too thin," "awkward," or even "geeky" during adolescence. It is only after "Being Discovered" (a life-altering process set normally at the beach or mall and usually initiated by a prominent fashion photographer) that these Hipsters are recognized, praised, and heavily compensated for their now all-too-obvious good looks. Pre-Discovery tales provide particularly good fodder for late-night television interviews.

---

*Male specimens do exist and are actually quite common. However, the female of the species is dominant and more worthy of serious field pursuit.

Raison d'être:

The primary function of these Hipsters is to look good and to, at times, stretch the very definition of what may be considered attractive [e.g., the respective heydays of Grace Jones, Kate Moss, et al.]. Constantly re-molded by a phalanx of specialized personal groom technicians, the species displays no consistent look, yet its willowy and transcendent figures are a dead giveaway. *Foreign-born specimens may prove especially heartbreaking to encounter.*

Models suffer from an insatiable desire to be photographed. When coupled with their lack of responsibility and resultant dearth of non-social scheduling, these Hipsters are visible to the point of oversatura-tion. It has been postulated that the species' need for photographic representation functions as the direct inverse to some primitive peo-ple's belief that picture taking steals one's soul.

Transference of Sex Appeal:

Models possess the unique ability to bestow shades of their own fabu-lousness upon objects with which they come in contact. Through sim-ple association, Models can transform otherwise unremarkable terrain into practically impenetrable hot spots and decidedly bland (yet wealthy) males into figures of pure sexual intrigue. *If one has the means, dating a Model is highly recommended.* Of course, this ability is merely an outgrowth of the species' well-known talent for lending articles of clothing, jewelry, or fragrances a hint of the must-have.

Brain Power:

The species' lack of intellectual prowess has been exhaustively docu-mented. Despite certain exceptions to the rule [e.g., Cindy Crawford, Brooke Shields, etc.], Models are among our less mentally gifted Hip-sters. The species compounds this shortcoming through its proclivity to speak publicly on issues of politics, philosophy, and science, thus vi-olating the common Hipster practice of discoursing only on subjects of immediate concern [e.g., Hippies limit most conversations to bong construction technique, drum circle theory, and female armpit hair rationalization].

Natural Enemy:
The species' status is at times threatened by their one natural enemy, the Socialite (*Trustfundium Celebutantas*). Obsessed with the concept of status, Socialites constitute the highest level of societal ranking, having inherited their fathers' wealth and family name along with their mothers' trophy wife looks. They are fabulous, fabulous sub-Hipsters and, as such, provide fertile fodder for observation, if only through more advantageously appointed intermediaries [i.e., "Page Six" of the *New York Post*].

A shared dating pool [i.e., Celebrities, Athletes, Scions, Male Models, Upper-Echelon Social Types, etc.] ensures ample opportunity to clash. Socialites tend to sniff at Models' lack of pedigree and limited shelf life. However, certain Socialites choose modeling as a "career." Though lovely, their success in the field is often attributed more to lineage than comeliness [e.g., Amanda Hearst, Lydia Hearst, Lauren Bush, etc.].

Habitat:
Most Models originate in terrain of little sociological interest, such as small midwestern towns, French seaside villages, or remote African districts. Once discovered, most specimens are hurried off either to New York or Los Angeles, or to fashionable European terrain such as Paris or Milan. Eventually, these Hipsters engage in a standardized loop of high-powered partying during which, velvet rope permitting, they are considered ripe for observation.

In Los Angeles, CA:

AVALON BAR *(9400 West Olympic Boulevard, Beverly Hills)*—After an "exhausting" day being "photographed" and drinking "bottled water," this "sexy" hotel lounge is better than "a weekend in Monaco." The poolside locale is perfect for "sipping a drink" with "Toby" or discussing "personal trainers" and, though some describe the scene as "sybaritic," most regulars say "What does that mean? I don't know that word."

BAR MARMONT *(8171 Sunset Boulevard, West Hollywood)*—"Featuring" apple martinis more "stylish" than "Stella McCartney" and salmon rolls that "Karl Lagerfield" used to "gorge on" before he "got thin," this "funky" hotel bar is noted for "statuesque" drink prices and a reputation that's "very now." Even "waifs" love the adjacent hotel, which is "fabulous" for a "quick bang with a rock star."

In New York NY:

B BAR *(40 East Fourth Street)*—Whether "brunching" or "clubbing," "strike a pose" at this still-hot spot where "she's going to catch me staring at her, but I can't help it." There's nothing like Tuesday night's Beige party for "making me wish my girlfriend was hotter" or "bribing the doorman to get in." Locals say "Haven't I seen you in the Hamptons?"

COFFEE SHOP *(29 Union Square West)*—"I'm only doing this temporarily," note members of the "gorgeous" wait-staff as they "sashay" their way to your table. Always reliable for people watching, this "glorified diner" is not renowned for "good food" or "mental prowess." Regulars recommend "humoring" the "attitude" of your "malnourished" waitress, as she "isn't getting any younger."

PERFORMANCE POETS

BLOVIATUM DRAMATICA

DREADLOCKS

FUEL

"POETRY"

The most narcissistic of all Hipsters, Performance Poets not only journal their rage but read it aloud, disseminating the details of their personal lives through a plangent, staccato, sometimes musically accompanied howling referred to as "Spoken Word."

A personal or anecdotal brush with trauma is normally required before one may be accepted by this species. Preferred topics include sex, anger, politics (liberal), racism, and sexual identity. As one time-tested intrascene saying puts it, there are three types of poems: Screw You, Screw Me, and Screw the Man. *White, straight males of non-Hip lineage, you have been forewarned.* Regrettably, a New Agey spin often obscures the depth of subjects plumbed.

Survival of the Fittest:
Performance Poets are among the most fiercely competitive of our Hipsters, regularly submitting themselves to vicious contests referred to as "Slams," in which performers are paraded before, then judged by, a roomful of latte-sipping iambic pentameter junkies. Though ostensibly based both on quality of poem recited and delivery, judges' marks usually reflect more on the performance than the written aspect. Preceded by a period of mortifying nervousness, "Open Slams" are the venues at which beginners first take flight after which, positive marks permitting, Hipsters are invited back to participate in more prestigious, invitation-only Slams. Performance Poets capable of competing in such rarified terrain win respect and sexual favors from the herd.

Mating Rituals:

As is the case with any performing species, these Hipsters possess huge sexual appeal. Fortunately for all involved, their inflated attractiveness lingers on in the moments directly following the completion of a set. Even mediocre performances (and there are many) are rewarded with an encore of intense sexual flirtation and eventual pairing off. The species regards this coital freewheeling as something of compensation for artistic services rendered, in lieu of cash money. Performance Poets allude to this state of professional affairs with the motto "If I'm not gonna get paid, I'm gonna get laid."

Habitat:

These Hipsters are best observed in cafés or barrooms hosting Open Mic Nights or Poetry Slams. Those venturing into such terrain are advised to never be without either a mug of coffee or bottled beer (preferably of domestic origin). In addition, seasoned observers have perfected the act of periodic head nodding, a gesture which, when refined, may suggest both intellectual appreciation and a personal connection to subjects plumbed.

> *In Atlanta, GA:*
> PARADIGM ARTSPACE ["SLAM CITY!"] *(1123 Spring Street)*—"Outside / alfresco as it were we gather / Courtyard stars in splendor shine on those / determined / abetted by lack of cover / free / of charge / to witness a spectacle / gaze upon one standing, preaching without sermon / yet strong of voice / artists of all kinds / disciplines / fretting / weighted down by concerns / practical / chained down / find here sweet relief like-minded souls / snacks / before again, too soon, away."

> *In Boston, MA:*
> NEW WORDS BOOKSTORE *(186 Hampshire Street, Cambridge)*—"Female, I am we are, who writes and here sells shops reads purchases with hard earned, Labor, sweat on my brow my culture muddled and multi, a place a spot to call our own, to accept us huddled without reproach, without the tyranny of stronger sex. Our home, our bosom. Not to be compromised or clumsily pawed like so many backseat fumblings, from whence we were, now free."

In New York, NY:
NUYORICAN POETS CAFÉ *(236 East Third Street)*—"Don't, she said as I slinked / up and out / the night beckoning / through Paned Glass. Cold. / I ran tears not knowing looking back through haze / to times unknown till here / I stumble, clasping walls, balance, unsure / but never wondering, ever / if anything, some diversion will be carried out / It always is / this institution full of comfort / and serenity beer and wine / I slam and hope to win or else forget / Until next week."

In Seattle, WA:
SIT & SPIN ["SEATTLE POETRY SLAM"] *(2219 Fourth Avenue)*—"I hearken to the days of forebears, where stream and stones rubbed smooth conspired, to break backs, backs broken, to here, now, where hope and detergent spring eternal, where that lassoed elemental force soothes and comforts, removing all trace of dirt and sweat. Electro! While others, content, consume baked goods measured, by diameter, in inches or try, sometimes desperately, to establish tangible connection before all is dried. You talk, I'll fold."

URBAN MOMS

FECUNDIA ADORABLUM

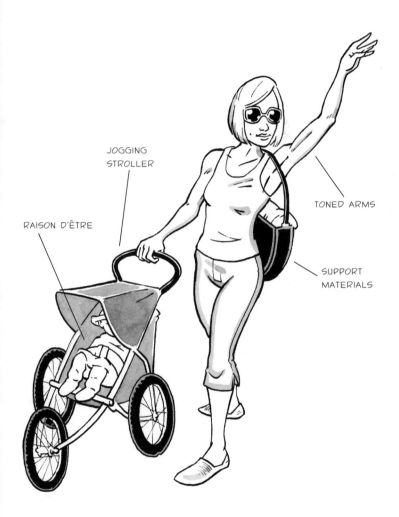

JOGGING
STROLLER

RAISON D'ÊTRE

TONED ARMS

SUPPORT
MATERIALS

EXTERIOR: Cargo capri pants; tank top; sculpted arms; nice belly; flip-flops; sandals; jogging shoes.
ACCESSORIES: Child; canine; iced chai latte.

Preposterously cute, these Hipsters are noted for a disarming ability to foster episodes of frantic lifestyle review in their less fortunately engaged observers [e.g., "Why don't we have children?"]. *Do not panic.* They are highly advanced in terms of biological makeup and leisure activity, and one should not measure one's own happiness against theirs.

For purposes of classification, it should be noted that nonrural address and pregnancy/child does not necessarily an Urban Mom make. We are concerned only with the Hip variety; that is, with Urban Moms who exhibit artistically employed husbands [e.g., graphic designer, musician, artist, architect], downtown leanings (figuratively or literally, depending on terrain), and Veronique maternity clothing [as opposed to, for example, Liz Lange].

Urban Moms are also fascinating for the speed with which they are able to rejuvenate their physiques immediately following childbirth. While less-fortunate specimens wrestle with the horrors of stretch marks, varicose veins, and public schools, Urban Moms exhibit the mysterious ability to appear in enviable shape mere hours after delivery.

By Day:
While certain specimens continue to work from home, the majority opt for more traditional, single-income domestic situations. This being the case, most fill their days with intricate schedules of regimented leisure. Both pre- and post-delivery, exercise is a staple of their daily routine and the "gym" is the center of the Urban Mom's social universe. The species is particularly fond of ultra-trendy activities such as yoga and

the excessively fashionable yogalates. Yoga is performed both through-out pregnancy and immediately thereafter.

When not exercising, Urban Moms make daily migrations to area parks. Preferably, this terrain will feature both playground equipment and designated dog-running facilities, as the species is noted for its in-sistence on both infant and canine companionship. Urban Moms re-fuse to associate with mixed abominations such as the unusually horrid German Shepherd/Border Collie combo and prefer instead to select from any number of trendy and ornamentally superior types [e.g., Ridgebacks, Bulldogs, etc.]. The species will, however, usually accept husbands of mixed ethnicity.

By Night:
Unlike those of their Uptown, non-Hip cousins, the species' mates are frequently present during the evening and are, consequently, quite in-volved in family life. While babysitter-assisted dining remains quite popular, the centerpiece of the Urban Mom's nocturnal repertoire is the Evening Spent at a Friend's Apartment. Such events typically involve wine sipping, cheese munching, baby rocking, vintage couch reclining, and mixed CD playing. Set exclusively in well-decorated and designer-catalogue-strewn apartments, these gatherings also provide a setting for ample quantities of nauseatingly sweet baby talk and the irritating scolding of dogs.

Herd Mentality:
Though members of a herd species, Urban Moms stick together more out of communal shared interest (and free time) than nontolerant ex-clusivity. In fact, childless acquaintances are encouraged to remain "in touch" and generally do, though most ultimately experience fatigue brought about by incessant childcentric rumination.

Branding:
In keeping with their image-conscious lifestyle, these Hipsters insist on naming their offspring from a constantly updated pool of acceptable

designations. Currently, fashion dictates names reeking of American stability and old-fashioned, grandparenty good tidings [e.g., Damien, Ethan, Ian, Jude, Stella, Colin, Sadie, Olivia, Jack, Henry (or the double shot Jack Henry), et al.]. Conversely, such saccharine embarrassments as Hannah and Tiffany are currently experiencing something of a widespread backlash.

Habitat:
Ideally, the Urban Mom's preferred environment offers substantial amusement for both children and adults. Though specifics may vary, observers would do well to limit their efforts to such obvious terrain as playgrounds, cultural centers [e.g., certain forward-thinking Ys], or, where applicable, petting zoos.

In Los Angeles, CA:
BACK DOOR BAKERY *(1710 Silverlake Boulevard, Silverlake)*—"Settle down" for some homemade granola and cinnamon toast at this "adorable" gourmet "breakfast nook" that's "stroller friendly." Enjoy some "quiet time" by "feeding" the kids an "egglette" and making the "shush" sound "ad nauseam." This place is "so fun," some like it "even better than their nanny."

ROXBURY PARK *(471 South Roxbury Drive, Beverly Hills)*—Partake in some lawn bowling, croquet, or "wet nursing" in a perfectly "manicured" setting that helps remind some of "why I chose to stay at home and raise the children." "Kids" can "foster their creative sides" in the pirate ship–themed playground while "mommy" "sunbathes" with her friends and discusses "my husband's first-look deal at Paramount."

In New York, NY:
BHAVA YOGA CENTER *(638 East Sixth Street)*—For "infants" whose lives are "too stressful," this studio offers "meditation" and an ideal, "nurturing" environment for "Mother, Child, Mother's Girlfriends" bonding. Most "babies" seem to really appreciate the secular approach to "Yoga Asana" after a rough day of "nap time" and "burping." Some locals rave "'Ohm' was her first word!"

TOMPKINS SQUARE PARK *(East Tenth Street)*—Grab an "iced latte" from "Café Pick Me Up" and head over to this former "notorious" "drug lair" for a pleasant afternoon of "chitchat" and "child rearing." Kids can learn about "the birds and the bees" firsthand in the "dog run" or "practice safety" by ignoring the entreaties of "homeless crazies." Most regulars recommend the "playground" closer to Avenue A, as it's "less ethnic."

VIDEO HOS

BABYGOTBACKA KNOCKBOOTSUM

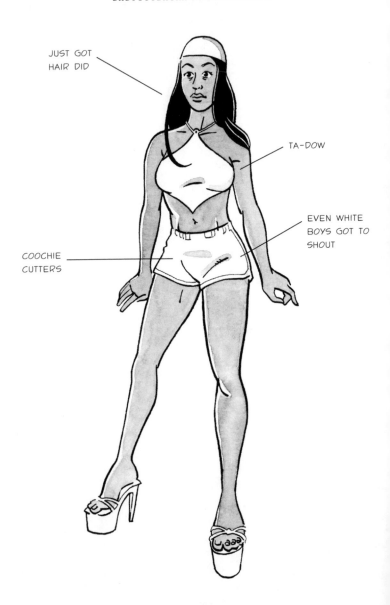

JUST GOT
HAIR DID

TA-DOW

EVEN WHITE
BOYS GOT TO
SHOUT

COOCHIE
CUTTERS

VIDEO HOS

EXTERIOR: Tight, skimpy, spandex clothing.
ACCESSORIES: Breast implants; long, multicolored fingernails.
PLUMAGE: Extensions; weave.

A lso referred to as "hoochies," this exclusively distaff species bears distinct similarities to their rock and roll cousins, the Groupie. As such, they are among the most sexually active and promiscuous of all Hipsters. Seemingly without noncoital merit, the species spends the majority of its time primping, preening, and shaking its collective posteriors, or "booties." Experts speculate that most specimens also undergo rigorous exercise regimens designed specifically for maximum spandex application capabilities. In emulation of gainfully employed music video dancers [*see* Jay-Z's "Big Pimpin'"], these Hipsters adopt a studied hookerlike appearance. Often involving some combination of breast implants, hair extensions, and tight clothing, the look is calculated to attract high numbers of affluent and celebrity-issue mates.

Raison d'être:

Though generally considered quite sexually inclined [i.e., "freaky"], Video Hos do exhibit nonamorous desires and a strong sense of societal determination. Many use sex as a means to attract the services of a so-called Sugar Daddy. Particularly toothsome specimens enjoy a high success rate. Once ensnared, this Sugar Daddy is obligated to provide his Video Ho with cash, clothes, cars, and an appropriate amount of fancy jewelry, sometimes referred to as "bling bling."

Competition:

Due to the limited number of available and noteworthy mates, Video Hos are an incredibly catty and competitive species. Furthermore, many lack a realistic appraisal of their own appearance. Such specimens, termed "skanks," though highly undesirable and something of a general annoyance, often insist on competing with and impeding the efforts of their more comely "sistas."

Habitat:

In Atlanta, GA:
CLUB 112 *(2329 Cheshire Bridge Road NE)*—"Get your dance on" at this "dirty South" institution that's "off the hook." A favorite among "skeezers who are on my jock 'cause I'm in showbiz," even the most "trick-ass bitch" raves "this place is on point." Whether "givin' skull" in the bathroom or "just chillin'" over by the bar, this club is "da bomb." Regulars insist, "he said he was with Snoop's entourage."

In New York, NY:
CLUB NEW YORK *(252 West 43rd Street)*—"He must be trippin'," complain "fine" patrons of this "Forty Deuce"–area club, where "sistas" "shake their rump" while avoiding "P. Diddy's" bullets. Though some "honeys" insist "I ain't hearin' that," "smooth" "macs" respond, "Come on, Girl, I'm just a squirrel lookin' for a nut." Remember, fellas, you "gots" to "get papers" before you can "score" some "punani."

The *Pickwickdon* Family

THREE SPECIES:

1. BIKE MESSENGERS

2. MODS

3. OUTLAW BIKERS

ALSO DISCUSSED:

1. BIKER CHICKS

2. RECREATIONAL BIKERS

Hipsters of this family, though not necessarily confined to their transports, are nonetheless most easily categorized by and most commonly spotted upon their two-wheeled vehicles of choice. By observing riding posture, it is easy to distinguish between these species [Figure 1].

A) OUTLAW BIKER   B) MOD   C) BIKE MESSENGER

BIKE MESSENGERS

CONDESCENDUM QUICKSILVERUS

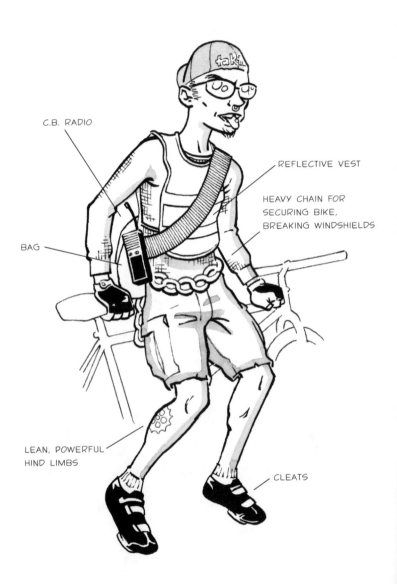

C.B. RADIO

REFLECTIVE VEST

HEAVY CHAIN FOR
SECURING BIKE,
BREAKING WINDSHIELDS

BAG

LEAN, POWERFUL
HIND LIMBS

CLEATS

EXTERIOR: Technical riding gear; army surplus; street clothing reimagined for bike riders (e.g., denim jeans with leg rolled up high on chain side); bike jersey; jacket advertising messenger company.
ACCESSORIES: Large, heavy Kryptonite chain draped over shoulder or worn as belt; messenger bag; text-message beeper, 2-way radio, or CB/cell phone hybrid.

B ike Messengers, though menial in function, exhibit an instinctual snobbery not normally observed outside of record stores or comic shops. Unlike their counter-dwelling cousins, whose attitudes are held in check by the confines of their environments, the Bike Messenger claims as its turf the very streets themselves, delivering the condescension, along with your package, to you. *Do not be intimidated. They are riding bicycles.*

This species, though Hip, is sometimes grouped with more generic, non-Hipster Bicycle Enthusiasts (*Waterbottlus Fannypackum*). As such, BMs often enter non-Messenger road races, profess knowledge of the European racing circuits, and align themselves with bicycle-friendly politics [*see* Natural Enemies, below]. Still, it is important to realize that BMs represent an extreme, cultlike end of the greater Cyclist spectrum.

Navigation:

Bike Messengers possess a sophisticated system of acoustic orientation referred to as "echo location." Operating at a frequency undetectable to normal human pedestrians, these Hipsters are able to disregard much of the information presented by their eyesight. Though not fully understood, experts believe that it is this talent which allows the species to operate with complete disregard for other forms of traffic or moving violations.

Breeds:
Two very distinct breeds of Bike Messengers have been identified.

1. **Refined**—The leg shaving (in emulation of pro racers, who do so for supposed wind-resistant purposes and as post-wipeout gravel entanglement prevention), frame polishing, nattily attired (by Messenger standards, i.e., spandex bike shorts, European racing jerseys, etc.). This breed normally rides road/racing bikes. Though more commonly associated with Enthusiasts, certain Messengers fit this description and are considered prized specimens.

2. **Common**—The tattooed, facially pierced, cargo pant wearing, heavy chain (to prevent bike theft) toting. This breed usually prefers mountain bikes and constitutes the typical, urban Bike Messenger [*see* main illustration].

Mating Rituals:
Owing to their swarthy noncorporate charms, Bike Messengers function as objects of desire for most office-dwelling Receptionists (*Coquettus Administratum*), who view the species through a certain veil of mystique. The relationship is mutually flirtatious, packages being retrieved and delivered against a backdrop of arched brows, furtive glances, excited giggles, and innuendo [e.g., "Sure, the men's room is just down the hall. Here's the key."]. The dynamic is perpetuated both by the BM's persistent adherence to favored routes and the modern business' reliance on a constant exchange of time-sensitive correspondence.

While not above casually reciprocating such workplace advances, Bike Messengers prefer their own kind for serious commitment. Though relatively uncommon, female Bike Messengers do exist and are often of spunky stock.

The Hive:

Bike Messengers are employed and controlled by courier companies. Often paid on commission (based on cost of delivery), it behooves them to make more and higher-profile (or urgent) deliveries. Deep within the labyrinthine walls of the courier company office lurks the Dispatcher (*Deskjockus Overweightum*), a creature responsible for every aspect of the BM's professional life and to whom he owes his allegiance. In charge of coordinating deliveries, the Dispatcher not only schedules the flights of his legions, but keeps in constant contact with each Worker via sophisticated airborne communication. Messengers strive to please the Dispatcher and win his favor, to be rewarded with more fruitful tasks.

Natural Enemies:

Though servants of the corporate world, Bike Messengers operate under a delusional belief that they are actually striving to undermine their true enemy, the Capitalist system. *Let them believe what they will; enjoy the speedy deliveries at which they excel.*

Capitalism aside, no predator strikes fear into these Hipsters like the automobile or, by extension, Automobile Drivers (*Inactivum Petroleus*). Bike Messengers exhibit a practically Amish aversion to all things automotive. Many believe that cars are anti-city and that expecting a city to endure automobile traffic as the exclusive or majorative user of its roads contradicts urban planning as it was truly intended [*see* Travis Hugh Culley's *The Immortal Class: Bike Messengers and the Cult of Human Power*].

Habitat:

While common in nearly all urban terrain, New York City, Chicago, Portland, OR, and San Francisco offer particularly fertile ground for observation. San Francisco, a veritable Bike Messenger haven, is the locale of many internationally attended BM events [e.g., The Cycle Messenger World Championships] as well as the home turf of the International Federation of Bike Messenger Associations (IFBMA).

In Chicago, IL:

CAL'S LIQUOR STORE *(400 South Wells Street)*—Cheap "skonskis?" "Roger." Ideal for a quick fix while "on standby" or a night of "nosmosis" for those not "holding" any "huffbo chente" in their "zo bag," one need not be a "gravy dog" to enjoy the cheap drinks and spend a few hours "talking out of a hole in my foot."

In New York, NY:

SOPHIE'S BAR *(509 East Fifth Street)*—Get drunk and commiserate over "boondas" and "donkeys" at this East Village bar featuring "milk" cheap enough to afford on "gristle." Play a little "Ms. Pac-Man" or pool, if you can beat the "civilians" to the table. The "scoobs" jukebox and delicious "light and darks" guarantee such a good time, you'll shut down your radio in order to avoid "last-minute dockets" from "Dick Scratcher."

In Portland, OR:

SHANGHAI TUNNEL *(211 SW Ankeny Street)*—This underground, smoky lair, though sometimes filled with "suits" fresh off their "penguin march," is ideal for "aggro" episodes inspired by "the tag catalyst" or drying off after a "messenger shower." Noodle dishes are highly recommended, but be sure to do a "10–200" before returning to the streets. Regulars note the plushy seats are perfect for soothing even the most painful "roadrash."

In San Francisco, CA:

ZEITGEIST *(199 Valencia Street)*—For "bike geeks" recently "doored" and enjoying a "messenger vacation," this bar/hotel provides an ideal setting for intimidating art students into doing the "funky chicken." Whether "top dog" or "muppet," patrons enjoy whiling away the hours discussing "the geist," deriding "techno weenies," or smoking a little "puff."

MODS

ANGLOPHILIA DANDYUM

1960S-STYLE SUIT

RIDES ON THE BACK

SCOOTER

IRONICALLY, STYLISH BOOTS NOT ACTUALLY MADE FOR WALKING

MODS

Male
EXTERIOR: Vintage, sharp, and "put together"; tight; fitted; well tailored.
By Day—Levi's denim "sta-prest" jeans; Fred Perry or Ben Sherman shirt; V-neck sweater; Lonsdale "Harrington" jacket (plain outside, plaid lining).
By Night—Three-button suit (jacket sometimes involves side vents) with matching trousers; skinny tie; dress shoes; green "fishtail" army parka.
PLUMAGE: Disheveled mop top.

Female
EXTERIOR: Early 1960s vintage.
By Day—Knee-length skirt; turtleneck; Mary Janes; stockings.
By Night—1960s shift dress (A-line with geometric pattern); stockings; Mary Janes or white go-go boots; 1960s vintage Jackie O–style coat; double-breasted or leather trench coat.
PLUMAGE: Symmetrical bob with bangs cut directly above eyes.
MARKINGS: Sometimes heavily made up (eyeliner, shadow, mascara, or fake lashes).

Both Sexes
FLIGHT: Via two-wheeled, motorized scooters of Italian make.

Inhabiting a subculture concerned primarily with aesthetics, these semi-obscure Hipsters are noted for a propensity to expend vast quantities of money and time perfecting a desired look [*see* main illustration]. An effete and dandified species, Mods desire, above all else, to present a studied, predictable, and decidedly British countenance. This fashion zealotry normally results in a standard mix of tight, well-tailored clothing (male) or vintage dresses and frocks of the early 1960s (female).

Experts speculate that the Mod's refined sensibility and resultant lack of physical exertion has led to severe weakening of the muscles located in these Hipsters' hindquarters. As a result, many specimens find prolonged walking to represent a physical impossibility and require the assistance of specially designed vehicles. Usually referred to as a "Vespa," this two-wheeled contraption allows the Mod to maintain a regular schedule of Britpop club nights and *Quadrophenia* retrospectives without the risk of serious fatigue or bodily harm. Fortunately, the Vespa's sleek retro design allows this crutch to double, stylistically, as an accoutrement of equal standing to even the ubiquitous mop-top haircut.

Origin of the Species:
Though Mods have experienced several incarnations, casual observers interested in origin should focus on the earliest sightings, as each successive revival has represented a gradual watering down of the original intent, to the point where today's Mods possess literally no depth.

The species dates back to a group of middle-class, (mostly) Jewish London teenagers with connections to the garment trade in the waning years of the 1950s. Obsessed with personal style, these early specimens became enamored, primarily, with slim-cut Italian suits popular at the time. Music became the Mods' other defining obsession. At first content to appropriate preexisting forms [e.g., modern jazz, ska, northern soul, rhythm and blues], these Hipsters ultimately created a sound more representative of their own effete sensibilities or gravitated toward bands already exhibiting a similar aesthetic [e.g., The Who, The Small Faces, The Kinks, The Pretty Things, The Creation, The Birds, John's Children, The Sorrows, et al.].

The Mod-Punk scene of the late 1970s is considered, by some aficionados, the high-water mark in regard to artistic output associated with these Hipsters. Spurned on by the music of The Jam and the release of The Who's seminal *Quadrophenia*, this period, though in some ways more fruitful than the original, remains a reworking of a previously established movement. As such, cursory familiarity with this epoch should suffice while in the field, though observers are encouraged to enjoy the work created therein [e.g., Secret Affair, The Chords, Merton Parkas, Squire, The Lambrettas, The Moment, Purple Hearts, etc.].

The Britpop phenomenon of the 1990s finally stripped the Mod of any remaining vestiges of substance. Essentially comprised of bands (and their fans) inspired by the species' incomparable style and reputation, Britpop disregards the traditional Mod sound while retaining timeworn motifs [e.g., Blur, Ocean Colour Scene, Oasis, Pulp, et al.]. While connoisseurs may point to some esoteric disparity between Britpop and Mod, the fact remains that bars or clubs hosting Britpop events represent the single most fertile terrain for observing this species. Such events, though usually listed in local entertainment weeklies, may also be recognized by outbreaks of parked motor scooters in the general vicinity.

Evolution:

In today's Hipster climate, it is very unusual for a specimen to assume a Mod persona directly; that is, from previously non-Hip affiliation. In other words, most Mods begin life as some other creature before evolving into a member of this species. Thanks to recent advancements in the field, experts are now able to postulate on precisely how this metamorphosis occurs. Two well-documented case studies, including natural progression, are noted briefly below:

1. **Rude Boy** → 1980s Ska → the Scooters → The Clash → The Jam → **Mod**
2. **Goth** → 1980s Goth → The Cure → The Smiths → Britpop → The Jam → **Mod**

Disposition:

Mods have been known to exhibit a demeanor which some experts regard as "a bit snooty." Technically open to anyone possessing even a modicum of good taste, certain undesirables, such as those unfortunate enough to have acquired, from their mother's side, a decidedly thick, wavy, and Hebraic follicular situation, are routinely castigated and made to feel somewhat unwelcome. Though free to gather in the general vicinity and even, on occasion, dance drunkenly to "Common People," official acceptance by the herd is reserved for thinner, taller, floppier-haired types.

Natural Enemies:

Though once the main rival of the generic Rocker, today's Mods seem content to prey upon the helpless Hippie, a pacifistic Hipster usually too "stoned" to engage in any serious violence [*see* entry]. It is through their very existence that these unkempt, dirty creatures find themselves the primary object of the Mod's refined scorn. Unwilling, or unable, to cloak themselves in high fashion or, much less, bathe, Hippies may remind the Mod of its long-shed working class roots.

On the other hand, Mods are often victimized, at least verbally, at the hands of their *Pickwickdon* superiors, the Outlaw Biker [*see* entry]. This large, aggressive Hipster seems personally and deeply wounded by the Mod's ability to ride, unembarrassed, upon such an effeminate and undignified conveyance as the scooter. In fact, the very word "scooter" is liable to inflame the nostrils of any Outlaw Bikers who happen to be in the general vicinity. Certain Mod specimens have even been observed approaching an Outlaw in an effort to praise the latter's bike. Such entreaties, though tolerated to a degree, have been known to culminate with a severe beat-down, delivered via skull-topped cane.

Habitat:

This species is best observed in terrain designated for its amusement. Usually located in environments featuring a rotating schedule of nightly themes [e.g., Glam Night, Goth Night, Love Night, etc.], the Mod's indigenous evening will likely either contain the phrase "Brit-pop" or have some vaguely 1960s or British connotation to its title. Though scarce and difficult to negotiate, this terrain is steeped in the highest level of dance music yet identified in the Hipster Kingdom. Therefore, observation is not only recommended, but *enthusiastically encouraged.*

In Boston, MA:

COMMON GROUND ["WHAT A WAY TO GO-GO"] *(85 Harvard Avenue, Allston)*—Stop off at "the chemist" for a pack of "johnnies," as regulars at this club have been known to get "jammy." Though some "cunts" had to "nick" the "two bob" for "a pint," even these "daft" "geezers" think the girl doing "the pony" to "Get Off of My Cloud" is "a bit of all right."

In New York, NY:

DON HILL'S [" 'TISWAS"] *(511 Greenwich Street)*—For those who "fancy" blowing "ten quid" at the door before getting "pissed" with their "mates," this "brilliant" Saturday night party is a real "giggle." Whether lip-synching "Parklife" on stage or "blabbing me mouth off" to a cute "bird" from Jersey, "lads" and their "blokes" say it's "more fun than a Bank Holiday."

In Salt Lake City, UT:

URBAN LOUNGE ["READY, STEADY, GO"] *(241 South 500 East)*—"We are the Mods," chant "porkpie hat"–wearing locals at this "barmy" hotspot that's "more my cup a tea" than "polygamy." Though "greasers" say "F off," those with the right "gear" realize that "Rockers" are "pure rubbish." Regulars "buggered" from this conflict say "give us a break, right?" "Cheers."

In San Francisco, CA:

330 RITCH STREET ["POPSCENE"] *(330 Ritch Street)*—Jump on your "Lambretta," pop a few "amphetamines," and head over to this weekly event that's "bloody" "awright." Perfect for "remembering Keith Moon," "smoking fags," or "working on my British accent," even "skinny pale guys" with "largish noses" seem to score like it's "nuffing."

OUTLAW BIKERS

HARLDAVINUS REBELLINUS

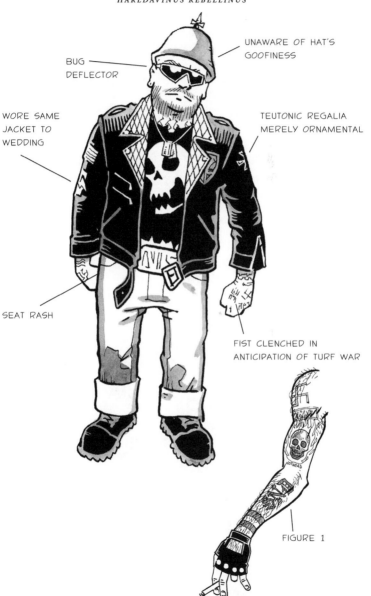

BUG DEFLECTOR

UNAWARE OF HAT'S GOOFINESS

WORE SAME JACKET TO WEDDING

TEUTONIC REGALIA MERELY ORNAMENTAL

SEAT RASH

FIST CLENCHED IN ANTICIPATION OF TURF WAR

FIGURE 1

EXTERIOR: Custom-made leather jacket emblazoned with club insignia; well-worn jeans; bike-themed T-shirt; leather boots.
ACCESSORIES: Iron crosses; assorted silver jewelry.
MARKINGS: Heavily tattooed.

The Outlaw Biker is one of the most dangerous Hipsters one may encounter in the field. *Approach with extreme caution, if at all.* In case of actual contact, a reverential tone is suggested. The species is similar to the Recreational Biker, yet is more organized, underemployed, dangerous, and tattooed [Figure 1].

FIGURE 2: DORSAL MARKINGS

Outlaw Bikers often travel in clubs, like wolves or debutantes. Dorsal markings distinguish club allegiance [Figure 2]. These marks may appear as skulls, flames, or witty slogans [e.g., "Honda Civic: From the

People Who Brought You Pearl Harbor"]. The Hell's Angels are the best known of these clubs and count many large metropolitan areas, such as New York City, as their turf. In this terrain, their Clubhouse is located on an otherwise charming block of Third Street between First and Second Avenues. If no alternate route is possible, walk briskly and keep your eyes averted. *Do not get caught peering at them through binoculars* [*see* Appendix II: Approaching a Dangerous Hipster]. Other clubs include the Pagans, Black Rebels, Warlocks, Vagos, and Diablos. Clubs like the Hell's Angels offer more than just street justice, knife fights, and frat house–style bonding. The Angels are a fully incorporated enterprise, specializing in T-shirts and concert security [e.g., *Gimme Shelter*].

Origin of the Species:
The Outlaw Biker is one of the few Hipsters to profess a philosophy other than shared fashion sense. The species was first discovered in post–World War II California, when returning veterans found themselves unable to shed their warrior trappings and pursue the American Dream. Instead, the original Outlaws bought bikes, "chopped" them [*see* below], donned memorabilia picked up in Europe (especially symbols of terror such as the swastika), and terrorized the local populous. Today, Outlaws are quick to point out that said symbols do not represent an actual adherence to any political system possibly suggested. *Thus, if a good friend begins dating an Outlaw with a penchant for Iron Crosses and you happen to be Jewish, do not take offense.*

Raison d'être:
The Outlaw usually rides a bike he has built himself or which has been custom-built for him. Thus, much of the culture revolves around local aftermarket bike shops, wherein motorcycles are assembled per order and Bikers gather to discuss engines and compare scars. "Choppers" are the requisite Outlaw machine. Though widely assumed to denote a motorcycle with comically elongated forks, "chopper" actually refers to any bike stripped down to only its essential parts. The most badassed chopper of all is the "rigid," named for the ride resulting from its missing

rear shocks. Riding a rigid in New York City is deemed to be "serious shit."

Related Hipsters:
Outlaw Bikers exhibit similarities to, or associate themselves with, several other species. Major examples include:

BIKER CHICKS (*Harldavinus Superfluousa*)—Entirely ornamental in function, these females (referred to, colloquially, as "Mamas") are most often observed perched upon the backs of motorcycles. They exhibit little autonomy or tangible depth, though do possess an innate ability to lean perfectly into corners. BCs are viewed largely as property.

RECREATIONAL BIKERS (*Harldavinus Yuppdork-Weekendicus*)—Wealthy professional types who enjoy playing Biker on the weekend, these sub-Hipsters prefer big, expensive cruiser bikes and tend to drape themselves in officially licensed Harley Davidson gear. They are not considered actual "Bikers" by Outlaws.

Habitat:
While New York and California offer the best terrain for viewing, Outlaws exist practically everywhere. Bike Weeks are extremely popular events, and are held in such cities as Myrtle Beach, Daytona Beach, Sturgis, Laughlin, etc. Also of note is California's Pacific Coast Highway as a whole (and Malibu in particular), which is favored cruising terrain.

In Los Angeles, CA:
ROCKSTORE *(30354 Mulholland Highway, Cornell)*—Ignore "the heat" and head up to this old "gin mill" for a nice dinner and possible helping of "fresh meat." The semiclassy atmosphere ("Look, it's Jay Leno") may discourage some women from "freeing their puppies," but even the most timid exhibit their "slutty" sides after "a few Buds."

In New York, NY:

AMERICAN TRASH *(1471 First Avenue)*—Feel free to "whip it out" in this humble "slice of Americana" that welcomes all types and prides itself on the recent addition of a lock to the women's bathroom door. You'll find plenty of "chicks" willing to "polish your knob" at this tribute to the days of old, when "America" was full of "Americans" and there were "no Japs," or "fat chicks."

HOGS & HEIFERS *(859 Washington Street)*—Packed with young college girls ready to be "groped" and "manhandled," this West Sider boasts hot bartenders, flying bras, and a "lead pipe–friendly" atmosphere. Perfect for "leering" at fellow patrons or discussing the finer points of "turf warfare."

In San Francisco, CA:

HOLE IN THE WALL SALOON *(289 Eighth Street)*—For those who enjoy "boys" as much as "bikes," this "campy" "queer bar" is a favorite among the city's "fruitier" types. "Leather" is a must, though some prefer "nudity." The "cheap beer" and "anal sex in the men's room" keep regulars coming back for more. If you like to "dance" or "fondle testicles," this "seedy" rock club should be "right up your alley."

The *Trendylium* Family

THREE SPECIES:

1. ALTERNABOYS

2. ALTERNAGIRLS

3. INDIE ROCKERS

Largely interchangeable, these species represent a recent revival of safe countercultural motifs. While strongly asserting their non-*Graecus* standing, these Hipsters remain unaware of their own similarly rigid uniforms and close circle of practically identical acquaintances. In terms of dress, this family is perhaps most susceptible to the dictates of popular trend. Still reeling from Grunge's demise, the species seem as yet unable to settle on a permanent sartorial countenance.

ALTERNABOYS

NERVANUM SLACKERIUS

IRONY
(GET IT?)

UNKEMPT

"WORK" JACKET
PURCHASED AT
OBSCENE MARKUP

VINTAGE T-SHIRT

KITSCH

ALTERNABOYS

EXTERIOR: Work jackets with orange interior; faded band T-shirt; low-top Converse sneakers; straight-leg Dickies pants.
ACCESSORIES: Black-framed eyeglasses; cotton sweatband; necklace or bracelet involving ball bearings; leather bracelet cuff; wallet chain; grommet belt; cigarettes (Marlboro Reds or Camel Lights).
PLUMAGE: Dirty, scruffy. Beard and sideburns possible.
POSTURE: Sloped, suggesting unnatural curvature of spine.
FLIGHT: Via skateboard or child's BMX bicycle.

Ten years past its prime, the clock is ticking fast on this species. *Immediate observation is recommended.* Many original specimens have already evolved into other, more definitive types [*see* Indie Rockers, Mods, Ravers, DJs, etc.].

The AlternaBoy's theoretical interest in the identifying characteristics of other species may further confuse things. For example, though AlternaBoys may profess profound passion for, say, filmmaking, their complete lack of sincerity separates them from Starving Artists [*see* entry]. As a general rule of thumb, AlternaBoys will not pursue their supposed interests with anything approaching seriousness. They might casually place a guitar in their bedroom, but will not make music their priority.

Antiquity:

AlternaBoys provide a cultural link to our collective Hipster heritage, having stubbornly resisted temptation to abandon the ideals or fashions of the general Grunge aesthetic of the early 1990s. Still influenced by period cultural harbingers [e.g., the Beastie Boys, the original *Details* magazine, Lollapalooza, *Reality Bites*, Douglas Coupland, etc.], the species has changed very little over the last decade. Wallet chains may in fact contain fewer links than ten years prior, but conceptually they remain quite similar. Likewise, these Hipsters have yet to fully abandon the now culturally mainstream black plastic eyeglass frames. It seems that though their once slightly subversive accoutrements have been co-opted even by the non-Hip [e.g., Ashleigh Banfield], AlternaBoys retain a spurious yet adamant appreciation of their own sartorial rebelliousness.

Gas Station Attendant Shirts and Their Relation to the Libido:
Strangely, AlternaBoys are virtual maestros of all matters sexual. That they enjoy an exact female counterpart certainly helps [*see* Alterna-Girls], though the flamboyantly attractive nature of said females helps this species remain the object of bitter resentment for many. With the exception of Mods [*see* entry], AlternaBoys attract the most heart-breakingly attractive women of all our Hipsters.

Recently, the Gas Station Attendant Shirt, long the species' most emblematic symbol of socioeconomic irony and virility, passed slightly out of fashion. As explained by Stephen Jay Gould's Theory of Punctuated Equilibrium [*see The Panda's Thumb: More Reflections in Natural History*], a species remains relatively unchanged for long periods of time and change, when it occurs, is rapid (by evolutionary standards). Thus, the Alternative world (both sexes) was wholly unprepared for the sudden fall from grace of this timeworn possession.

Females are also drawn to the species' supposed lackadaisical, ad hoc relation to hipness. AlternaBoys put forth a studied appearance of just having somehow rolled out of bed trendy. Their act is not having an act [*see* the movie *Singles*].

Disposition:
AlternaBoys are committed to lifelong yet extremely low-grade sadness. As with their artistic inclinations, this melancholy is for the most part theoretical and the result of a sort of inverse of wishful thinking. They are attracted to the concept of unhappiness yet find the actual state of despair personally unappealing. In many ways, AlternaBoys lost their cultural compass with the death of Kurt Cobain. This shot heard 'round the world left a huge void in the species' affected disillusion-

ment, as they found themselves without the alter ego through which they had entertained fantasies of their own destruction. With the concept of death no longer theoretical and with the precipice staring them down for real, the species found itself unable or unwilling to follow their hero into the void. They remain in stasis, their casual sadness intact but no longer progressive.

Web Design:

That these Hipsters did not die out long ago is a testament to the pseudoartistic cachet provided by a career in web design. Flooding this field like Albanian refugees, AlternaBoys managed to co-opt the fruits of corporate employment while remaining spuriously convinced of the intrinsic differences separating them from their most hated enemy, the Ex-Frat [*see* entry]. Working 9 to 5, AlternaBoys have learned to adapt their appearance while in office terrain, retaining a general counterculture flavor while technically adhering to the tenants dictated by Business Casual.* Hence the appearance of studded belts woven through the loops of Dockers khaki pants and the equally popular French blue dress shirt tucked in only on one side [Figure 1].

FIGURE 1

---

*Such specimens have recently begun contemplating both enrollment in an MBA program and the development of a drug problem.

Habitat:

The species is best observed in terrain boasting a determined "dive" quality well suited to their semitortured posturing. Be aware that their appearance often varies depending on the environment. AlternaBoys native to New York City, for example, have exhibited a tendency to evolve toward a more modern, postmillennial interpretation of Alternative [i.e., mesh-backed caps, functionless sweatbands, and slightly tighter jeans]. Specimens indigenous to terrain even slightly farther afield, however, retain a decidedly mid-1990s countenance; some reportedly display the temerity to still venture out-of-doors, in broad daylight, equipped with nose rings. Such cretins are considered both unworthy of prolonged observation and one corduroy jacket away from a cashier's job at Urban Outfitters.

In Boston, MA:

THE MODEL CAFÉ *(7 North Beacon Street)*—Half townie, half trendy, this Allston institution features "retro video games" and plenty of "chicks with jagged black hair." "Compare tattoos" or "play some tunes" on the jukebox before "contemplating a move to New York" or "debating the merits of a Flash class." "That guy over there was Juliana Hatfield's guitarist" note patrons sitting in the window booth.

In New York, NY:

MAX FISH *(178 Ludlow Street)*—Garish "like that Dali exhibit I caught at the Met," this Lower East Side watering hole is the perfect destination for those looking to "chat over pinball" or unwind after "a long day of vintage clothes shopping." "Here's a flyer for our next show, you should check it out" suggest patrons at the bar, while locals recommend the adoption of a "nonseasonal wool hat policy."

2A *(25 Avenue A)*—"Did I mention my double major in musical composition and bioengineering?" ask regulars on the prowl at this East Village lounge. The upstairs couches are "so chill" and perfect for "relaxing with a girl" or "strumming my guitar." The downstairs bar may be a bit cramped, but "those guys over there look like Strokes." "Dudes" in line for the bathroom rave "I've been pissing here forever."

In Philadelphia, PA:

THE STANDARD TAP *(901 North Second Street)*—Dark and inviting, this Northern Liberties hot spot allows scenesters to "indulge in some microbrews" without "feeling too Fratty." Pop thrills may be at a minimum, but "White Stripes on the jukebox" and appropriately "shaggy-haired waiters rocking tight T-shirts" lend counterculture cachet to this corner bar. The burgers are "hardcore," but some feel the "lack of little girls with tattoos" is a "real bummer."

ALTERNAGIRLS

URBANOUTFITTERUM ORNAMENTIA

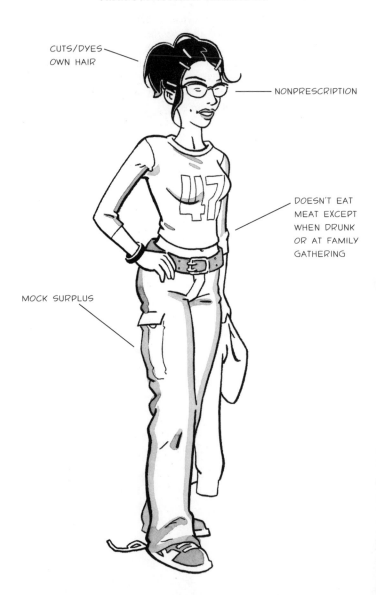

CUTS/DYES OWN HAIR

NONPRESCRIPTION

DOESN'T EAT MEAT EXCEPT WHEN DRUNK OR AT FAMILY GATHERING

MOCK SURPLUS

he female of this increasingly ubiquitous species is noted mainly for its vast arsenal of feminine wiles and the deliberate ease with which it ensnares male specimens. *They are very cute. Beware.*

These Hipsters exhibit chameleonlike qualities and will not hesitate to alter their appearance in keeping with the latest trends. Rest assured, however, that a general countercultural flavor remains constant despite their switching from, say, a camouflaged T-shirt to one bearing an ironically anachronistic slogan or from re-dyeing their red hair jet black and putting barrettes in it [Figure 1]. Positive identification may be further confused by intermittent applications of kitschy eyeglasses, though constant and flirty fiddling with said eyewear is a dead giveaway. Also

FIGURE 1: A SINGLE SPECIMEN EXHIBITS DIVERSE APPEARANCES

note the removal of these glasses during particularly furious bouts of journal writing.

Molting:

Studies indicate that many AlternaGirls have in fact spent a majority of their lives as blond-haired, perky All-Americans. Some have even been known to cheerlead. The Alternative gene is latent and usually manifests itself outwardly during the first or second year of undergraduate study. The Freshman Dorm serves as the cocoon in which this metamorphosis occurs [Figure 2]. During the chrysalis stage, in particular, a specimen may experience a tremendous rate of physical alteration, a phenomenon often referred to as the "freshman fifteen." Through exposure to trendiness and fashionable pessimism, the coed pupas are slowly and irreversibly transformed.

In extreme cases, these newly minted Hipsters will purposefully "lose" their freshman picture ID card, necessitating its replacement. This symbolic rebirth functions as both a declaration of self and a discarding

FIGURE 2

LARVAL STAGE   CHRYSALIS   FULLY DEVELOPED
                                             ALTERNAGIRL

of all evidence of the past. AlternaGirls will go to great lengths to assure you that they have "always been this way," even "before it was cool."

Mating Habits; Sexual Aggression:
AlternaGirls are unrelenting in their pursuit of so-called Cute Boys [*see* AlternaBoys, esp. "Gas Station Attendant Shirts and Their Relation to the Libido"]. They employ as their modus operandi a savvy reinterpretation of the little-girl-lost routine, in which they feign traditionally held assumptions concerning the "weaker" sex [e.g., an inability to master standard transmissions, author engaging student film scripts, heft kegs of beer up flights of stairs, etc.]. They flaunt their alienation through the establishment of a veritable culture based upon pouting [*see* the movie *Ghost World*]. Also of interest is the distinct possibility that much of this negativity is more a rejection of mainstream giddiness [*see* Alpha Females] than actual personal despair.

The pursuit of the fabled Cute Boy in a Band dictates much of the AlternaGirl's existence (in some cases, a Cute Boy on a Skateboard may be substituted). Many scientists remain puzzled regarding "The Cute Boy versus Quality of Music Played Ratio" [Figure 3], which states that the perceived quality of music played is equal and proportionate to sexual energy given off. *Buy a guitar.*

Oftentimes, AlternaGirls find themselves the objects of non-guitar playing boys' affections. These boys, despite whatever merits they may possess, have absolutely no shot of landing a trendy girlfriend and are doomed to lives of loneliness and despair [*see* author's photo].

Cachet of Poverty:
The fact that many AlternaGirls come from money clashes with their claims of disenfranchisement and must therefore be hidden. Unlike their natural enemies [*see* Alpha Females], who think nothing of living in comfort, AlternaGirls will only permit their parents to pay rent in slightly (or formerly) seedy districts. Thus they are afforded a hint of genuine urban grit and a carefree "watch me struggle" attitude. In other words: slumming.

FIGURE 3: AS A BOY IN A BAND'S "CUTENESS" INCREASES, SO DOES THE
PERCEIVED QUALITY OF THE MUSIC HE PLAYS.

Moreover, there exists an inverse relationship between the "coolness" of clothes worn and the amount of money spent on said clothes. That is, the cheaper the better. Typically overheard banter includes: "Ooh, I love those sneakers." "Thanks. I got them for $7." AlternaGirls will own up to the occasional designer purchase, but only with the preface "it was on sale."

Habitat:

These Hipsters are, on occasion, spotted in such nontrendy terrain as Manhattan's Theatre District or Upper East Side, usually as a result of some mainstream abomination along the lines of receiving tickets to *Les Misérables* for Christmas. They *will* alter their appearance to some degree for such excursions. While spotting them in such terrain may prove something of a challenge, the careful observer will take care to notice that (a) AlternaGirls retain a fastidious and palpable connection to their countercultural attitude [i.e., weary expression, cigarettes, bad skin, the rolling of eyes] regardless of actual appearance and (b) AlternaGirls will normally offset mainstream dress with some talisman of trend, e.g., Dr. Martens boots or facial piercing.

In Boston, MA:

ABBEY LOUNGE *(3 Beacon Street, Somerville)*—Unless "my boyfriend's playing tonight," save your cover money and head straight for the bar, where you can still hear the band while "pretending to be poor" at this "charming" dive that's "almost scary." "Bum a cigarette" from that "old guy on a stool," kiss a girl "just for fun," or simply sit back and appreciate "how good black hair looks with leopard print."

In New York, NY:

ODESSA *(117 Avenue A bet. 7th Street and St. Marks Place)*—You can "eat and drink, wow" at this venerable East Village institution that's "like so much cooler than diners in Jersey." A dark yet "flattering" lighting scheme, "skinny" bartenders with "messy hair," and a television set tuned "ironically" to football add up to make diners feel "conflicted, cute, and hungry all at once."

WELCOME TO THE JOHNSONS *(123 Rivington Street)*—"Bras are optional" at this Lower East Side homage to Kurt Cobain's "ancestral basement." Wood-paneled walls hung with vintage school portraits remind patrons of "the time Tommy Smith paused the Atari to feel me up." An "overzealous" heating policy ensures that "cute boys" will be "stripped down to their faded *Ghostbusters* T-shirts," while the "so-cheap" cans of Pabst Blue Ribbon are the perfect complement to your "white trash-esque" outfit.

In Philadelphia, PA:

SILK CITY LOUNGE *(435 Spring Garden Street)*—"I'm not sure what I want to do after school" note patrons at this hip Northern Liberties nightspot famous for its "adorable" DJs and "wardrobe-specific" theme nights, where dancing "is a perfect way to attract boys" and "makes up for not going to the gym." The bar is a perfect place to get "so messed up," though some wonder whether "camouflage is still in."

INDIE ROCKERS

AUDIOPHILUM INTEGRIA

TIMID

CARDIGAN

FALLS IN LOVE
TOO EASILY

FAVORITE STYLE
OF FOOTWEAR:
ORTHOPEDIC

INDIE ROCKERS

Male
EXTERIOR: T-shirt with band logo or of medium-tight thrift shop vintage (solid color, ironic iron-on); jeans.
ACCESSORIES: Canvas belt; messenger bag.
PLUMAGE: Semi bed-head.

Female
EXTERIOR: Skirt or jeans; T-shirt; Mary Janes; sneakers.

Both Sexes
FLIGHT: Via slightly used Volkswagen GTI.

N oted for elitism and misdirected precocity, these Hipsters profess stringent anticorporate/anticommercial ideals, yet the rabidity of these convictions does little to dilute their sensitive temperaments. They are musically obsessed and often condescend to those less familiar with the minutia of music released on independent rock labels, or "indie rock." These Hipsters often serve as clerks at small, independently owned record shops. *In such terrain, approach is strongly discouraged. Though cute and cuddly, they will strike with sardonic, cynical commentary at the first hint of dilettantism or ignorance.*

Origins of the Species:

As with other reactionary musical forms, it is easier to define indie rock by what it is not or, in this case, by what it rejects: commercial success, celebrity, fashion, sex appeal, zest. Velvet Underground provided the template in the 1960s. From there it drifted into the post-punk of the late 1970s/early 1980s [e.g., Elvis Costello, Talking Heads, the Pretenders, etc.] and through the college radio heyday of the mid- to late 1980s [e.g., R.E.M., U2, Camper Van Beethoven, etc.], when it was distinguished less by deviation from mainstream pop than by lack of an audience. College radio eventually developed a harder edge and became Alternative [e.g., Nirvana] until, with the explosion of the Seattle

Grunge scene, scenesters craved an alternative to Alternative: indie rock.

Evolutionary, success-based elimination is inherent to the species' survival. Many indie bands fall out of favor as they move from small, independent labels [e.g., Kill Rock Stars, Lookout! Records, Touch and Go Records, 4AD Records, K Records, et al.] to large, corporate entities.

Mating Habits:
Indie Rockers are sexually clumsy creatures. Their mating dance is an intricate yet ineffectual cocktail of lapsed intimacy, misread gestures, arcane trivia, and hero worship. It has been suggested that the species' heightened yet misguided intelligence often proves prohibitive to animalistic urges.

As a rule, Indie Rockers do not date. They fall in love, then break up through an often intense process normally set to particularly pretty and melodic music [e.g., Belle and Sebastian, Galaxie 500, Damon & Naomi, etc.]. These Hipsters engage in a perpetual cycle of exciting new prospective relationships and awful, devastating breakups.

Shoegazing:
These Hipsters are noted for a propensity to stare at their own feet during occasions of theoretical social interaction. Indie rock shows are a decidedly solitary affair; the herd listens to the music in absolute, compartmentalized silence. Occasionally, a Hipster may utter the phrase "This is so good," though such instances are extremely rare. In an act of social malfeasance on a par with falling asleep at a party [see Goths], Indie Rockers sometimes remain seated, primly, during a show's entirety.

To further discourage conversation, bands are often accompanied by visuals such as abstract video projections or amateurish art displays. Such aids not only hinder contact, but provide emotional clues as well. The combination of clever lyrics and profound visuals allows each Indie Rocker to ascertain precisely which emotion should be derived from each performance.

Habitat:

These Hipsters spend the majority of their time in the safe confines of record shop terrain, an environment perfectly suited to their penchant for pompous opinionating. Such locales may feature events such as in-store concerts, CD release parties, or socially desperate gatherings known as CD listening parties. Novice observers, however, would do well to limit their excursions to the slightly less forbidding bars and clubs preferred by the species.

In Athens, GA:
THE 40 WATT CLUB *(285 West Washington Street)*—Despite tangible links to such "overproduced" "sellouts" as R.E.M., this musical "space" appeals to even the most "cynical" local scenesters. Whether just dropping by to "check out that math rock band" or working on a feature article for your "Zine," this "essential" bar is "as influential as Thurston Moore" and boasts a clientele practically as "precocious" as *"Slanted and Enchanted."* "Sensitive" types may "dismiss" the occasional hip-hop show, though violence is usually averted thanks to the fact that "I don't know how to punch."

In New York, NY:
NORTHSIX *(66 North Sixth Street, Williamsburg, Brooklyn)*—Featuring "great acoustics," high school gym–esque bleachers, and a fish tank "I read about in *Alternative Press*," music lovers flock to this "seminal" Brooklyn venue. Though relatively new, bathrooms with more breadth than "Yo La Tengo's catalogue" and two competing stages "in the tradition of Lou Barlow" have helped the bar become popular "faster than The Shins sold out." While a DJ room is also featured, its contributions are often "more overshadowed than Kim Deal's."

In Philadelphia, PA:
700 CLUB *(700 North Second Street)*—Tighter than "Pollard and Sprout's early work," this converted house can get "more crowded than Polyphonic Spree's dressing room" after 10:00 P.M., when DJs start spinning a "credible" mix of "retro" "psyche pop" and "Young MC" to a crowd of "white guys with Afros" and overheated dancers who "smell worse than my old Pumas." Don't forget your ID; the "slouching" doorman turns underage kids away faster than "Sleater-Kinney rejecting a Lollapalooza invite."

In St. Louis, MO:

ROCKET BAR *(2001 Locust Street)*—This dive is renowned for a jukebox with "more cred" than "a one-night stand with Lou Reed" and "7-inch" beers guaranteed to "knock you out" faster than "I snatched My Bloody Valentine's *Loveless* out of the used bin." Live music is an added attraction, but don't forget your "low-top All-Stars" and "cuffed jeans" if you hope to score with "that emo girl" with "horn-rims and pigtails."

Accidental Species

THREE SPECIES:

1. FUNCTIONING JUNKIES

2. INTERNET GEEKS

3. THE LIFER

Accidental species are relatively rare Hipsters who do not breed regularly or occur annually in North America, but whose presence has been accepted by the American Hipthologists' Association (AHA). The following species have been photographed in the field at least once, though knowledge of their existence is based largely on anecdotal evidence. Normally indigenous to non-Hip terrain, certain solitary specimens do wander into officially recognized environments on occasion.

FUNCTIONING JUNKIES

ADDICTIVA RATIONALIZUM

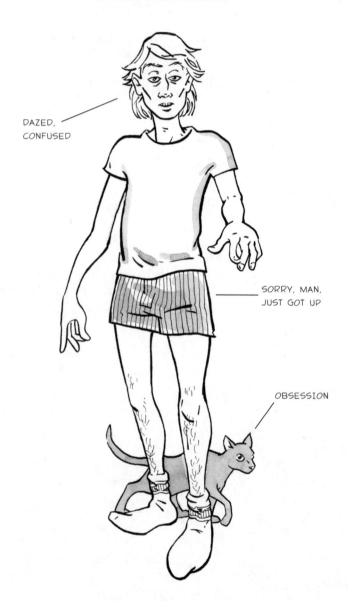

DAZED,
CONFUSED

SORRY, MAN,
JUST GOT UP

OBSESSION

FUNCTIONING JUNKIES

EXTERIOR: Nondescript; comfortable; pajama bottoms; boxers; T-shirts; thick socks.
PLUMAGE: Longish and slightly greasy.
ACCESSORIES: Sunken or hollow eye sockets; baggies; twist ties.
VOICE: Either incessant flutelike chattering or waning and slurred gurgling.

A loose-knit and sprawling species, Functioning Junkies expend great effort maintaining an illusion of drug-free independence. However, the spastic energy with which they pursue this endeavor lends their designs on normalcy a manic and fevered tinge. The species prides itself on episodes of personal interaction, through which it attempts to achieve some level of validation. In reality, however, the practice yields little, save for bewilderment on the part of its recipients. These Hipsters are peerless in their ability to unintentionally amuse.

Functioning Junkies differ from their more generic brethren [i.e., Junkies] not in the amount of illicit drugs ingested, but in an unwillingness to give themselves over entirely to the practice. While some experts suggest that FJs possess a higher level of physical tolerance, most discount this theory in favor of nurture over nature. A majority of Functioning Junkies are bred by upper-middle-class and otherwise respectable families. While often dysfunctional in their own right [e.g., alcoholism, prescription drug addiction, country club participation, et al.], these elders are not so far removed from reality as to withdraw completely from the lives of their offspring. The near-constant threat of parental visitation and subsequent disapproval (and disowning) inspires most Functioning Junkies to at least keep up appearances. Theirs is a highly evolved and adaptable species.

The Den:

Functioning Junkies are renowned for an instinctual ability to accrue enviable quantities of home electronics, decorative items, and clothing. Due to an often severely agoraphobic constitution, the species spends considerable time in the privacy of its own apartment, usually in the supine position. Given their refined tastes, these Hipsters require a steady cash flow. While certain specimens are functional enough to maintain actual employment, the majority opt for a somewhat less orthodox, yet fitting, career path, namely the dissemination of non–FDA-approved pharmaceuticals.

The species is also noted for a fanatical reliance on services of home delivery [e.g., the now sadly defunct Kozmo.com]. This devotion not only increases time spent in the home but capitalizes upon the FJ's penchant for esoteric and sudden cravings. By removing physical effort and the constraints of business hours from the equation, these Hipsters may more easily alleviate their overwhelming need for objects advertised on late-night television, munchies, and technology [e.g., DVDs, digital cameras, stereo equipment, video game consoles, etc.].

Disposition:

The species does not exhibit a uniform disposition. Instead, each specimen's manner is dependent upon his or her drug of choice. Common behavioral characteristics are listed below, according to drug of choice:

COCAINE—Extremely talkative and possessing an ability to ruminate on literally any subject. Inability to gauge the reaction of others. Very excitable.

HEROIN—Mellow to the point of being incommunicative. Personality similar to that of a melted Popsicle. Often literally unaware of the presence of others. Exist in a constant state of near hibernation, broken up by short, periodic episodes of manic fidgeting.

MARIJUANA—Varies. Certain specimens exhibit feelings of intense paranoia; others are prone to fits of hysterical giggling; still more exude spaced-out, blandly Zen-like dispositions. All accompanied by a comically intense desire to consume food products and ruminate deeply on shallow subjects.

Fixations:

Functioning Junkies are often held rapt by decidedly mundane objects and events. Articles known to foster feelings of concentrated affection, such as kittens, will engender nonhealthy levels of obsession in these Hipsters. Such objects become the center of their universe and will proceed to be featured, quite heavily, in all future conversations regardless of time, place, or pertinence. Once a Functioning Junkie has settled on a fixation, he is unable to disengage and is likewise insensitive to looks of sheer boredom or attempts to change subject. *They will regale at will; resistance is largely futile.*

Habitat:

Observation of these elusive Hipsters can prove quite challenging, as personal invitation is often required. Aside from actually befriending a FJ (*not recommended*), certain ruses may yield acceptable results. Posing as a customer, for example, has been known to reap the benefit of entry, though certain dangers are inherent to such infiltration, especially where a Hipster hooked on hard drugs is involved. Assuming a temporary position as pizza delivery boy may result in occasional contact without risk of bodily harm or imprisonment, though compensation is often scandalously low.

In the Living Room:

THE COUCH *(Four feet away from television)*—Take a long day's journey into "the depths" of "my amazing DVD collection" or conduct a "borderline manic" love affair with "NPR." "My girlfriend left, I think, yesterday," but despite the "crippling loneliness," locals "keep the ringer off" in order to avoid "accusations" from their "Jewish parents."

On the Stoop:

THIRD STEP *(From bottom)*—Take a 3 A.M. "constitutional" at this favorite spot for "dozing off," contemplating a "walk to the all-night pharmacy" for "Visine" or simply "staring absently" into the distance. Whether "hanging out with the super" or contemplating a "temp job" in order to "keep up appearances," the convenient location and "helpful handrails" add up to "primo" "vegging out."

In the Bedroom:

THE BED *(On top of covers)*—This normally cozy locale is perfect for "sticking out a cold sweat" or a nasty case of the "shivers." Though occasionally used for "sex with that girl from the movie theatre," most activity is limited to "fumbling for seeds" or "hallucinating." Heavy blinds provide a welcome respite from "that horrible Sun," while the lack of an alarm clock allows adequate recovery from "the four straight days I sat up staring at playoff hockey."

In the Bathroom:

TILE FLOOR *(In front of toilet)*—Settle in for a long night of "dry heaves" interspersed with the occasional "leg cramps" brought on by the "rock"-hard tile floor. Some regulars "wish I were dead," while others attempt to "keep some soup down" that was made earlier in "these really fancy and expensive pots I bought online." Once the night ends, "I'm definitely getting clean." "For real this time."

INTERNET GEEKS

DARTHIS DORKAM

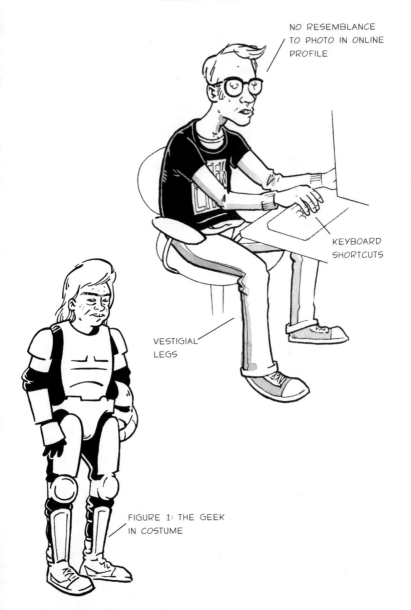

NO RESEMBLANCE
TO PHOTO IN ONLINE
PROFILE

KEYBOARD
SHORTCUTS

VESTIGIAL
LEGS

FIGURE 1: THE GEEK
IN COSTUME

Combining a startling lack of melanin with an instinctual fear of the outdoors (and exercise), this species is noted, physically, for its pasty complexion and a strange ability to appear either pudgy or gaunt.

Since access to the Internet is vital to the species' survival, most IGs are either students or employed in some sort of Internet Technology (IT) capacity. Female Internet Geeks do exist, and their small numbers (estimated at 5 percent of the IG population) make them quite a valuable commodity. They are traditionally forgiven transgressions that would result in brutal Flaming [*see* below] for a male [e.g., posting a theory that Mace Windu, not Anakin Skywalker, becomes Darth Vader in Episode III].

Usernames:

Internet Geeks are a faceless species, recognized only by their adopted sobriquets, called "Usernames," of which two main categories exist:

1. Internet Geeks who assume the identity of their Usernames (usually a favorite fantasy character) while posting.

2. Internet Geeks who employ a Username as a method of posting anonymously. This Username usually offers some insight into its user's personality or likes/dislikes [e.g., DarthPatrick, GrandMoffNaughton, etc.].

Raison d'être:

Like Academics [*see* entry], Internet Geeks live for the thrill of endless and meaningless debate. Their concerns are generally so pedantic as to completely blur the larger picture. No greater fodder for debate exists than the *Star Wars* saga. With the eventual six movies, their respective screenplays, countless novels, encyclopedias, interviews given by participants, etc., an unbelievable amount of information on the subject exists, thus creating an infinite number of issues to be argued over [e.g., "How can Obi-Wan have the same light saber in *Attack of the Clones* when he clearly lost it near the end of *The Phantom Menace*?"]. These debates take on a very real-world quality for Internet Geeks, as there is very little sense that the subjects being debated are fictional.

Communication:

Internet Geeks must exhibit one defining love or hate [e.g., *Star Wars* versus *The Lord of the Rings*]. This subject functions both as a means of expression and as an entrée into any existing post string. An overwhelming Bash/Gush Quotient dictates the culture. Postings are overwhelmingly positive or negative and are often distinguished by hyperbole bordering on the embarrassing; minute alterations to time-worn conventions are said to have "raped my childhood," while rumors of artistic liberty are met with hollow threats of suicide or murder.

Costumes:

Internet Geeks do occasionally log off from their computers and congregate in public. IGs appearing in costume are termed "Flamboyantly Geeky" [Figure 1]. The act of costuming is taken very seriously and entire web sites are devoted to their precise construction [e.g., http://www.tatooine.fortunecity.com/swampthing/97/]. Costumes are usually donned for participation in some Geek-approved event or other, such as waiting in line for *Star Wars* tickets.

Habitat:

AIN'T IT COOL NEWS *(www.aintitcool.com)*—"Fanboys" with nothing better to do scream "firsties!!!" at these "Talk Back" boards, where some discover a sense of spirituality by "praying" that "someone beats Akiva Goldsman to death with his *A Beautiful Mind* Oscar" for "destroying the *Batman* franchise!!!" Check your optimism at the door, because everything "freaking sucks!" including "Harry," who "can't spell or construct a sentence for crap!"

THEONERING.NET *(www.theonering.net)*—Select a "Dwarvish name" and apply your "pointy ears" before logging on to discuss the "feeble-mindedness of Tooks" while awaiting "Gandalf's return." Whether pondering literature in the "Tolkien room" or pitting "Billy the Pony" against "Aslan the Lion" in the "arena," a lack of humor is essential, as questions pertaining to the "physical composition of Elrond's sword" must be addressed with the seriousness of "Bilbo Baggins."

THEFORCE.NET *(www.theforce.net)*—Visitors to the "Jedi Counsel" debate whether or not "Luke had a mullet in *A New Hope*" or if "★ N Sync made it into the final fight scene in *Attack of the Clones.*" This is the perfect locale for those who "have seen the original trilogy at least twenty times" and would like to "discuss Episode III" with "spoilers." While some ponder "the ability of light sabers to cauterize wounds," others prefer to sit back and "lament the fact that George isn't hip anymore."

NEWS ASKEW *(www.newsaskew.com)*—"Snootches," note visitors to this gathering place for discussion of "all things geeky" and the "witless" retorts that follow. "There is absolutely no way" that "Jeremy London" doesn't "suck," claim regulars who lament "the destruction of the animated *Clerks* series" and lust over "my Jason Lee screensaver." "Kevin is totally selling out" by "shooting *Jersey Girl* in Philadelphia," but at least these message boards are "kind of like dating."

THE LIFER

SOLITARUM ESLOCO

SEEN IT ALL

ALCOHOL

LEATHERY HIDE

OBSCURE,
DEFUNCT
BAND

THE LIFER

EXTERIOR: Wizened countenance; mysterious dent in forehead or other strange physical feature; ancient concert T-shirt; jeans.
PLUMAGE: Long; white; balding.

Unique in that it does not belong to a species which congregates, or even acknowledges, one another, The Lifer is the only Hipster that remains completely ignorant of its classification as such. While generally not Hip, nor young, the species warrants inclusion due to its impressive ability to peacefully coexist in otherwise trendy terrain. *Approach is unnecessary; they will initiate conversation when ready.* Most specimens tend to be between 53 and 65 years of age, with little reported deviation.

The Lifer is rarely spotted outside of a drinking establishment. Interestingly, only one Lifer is allotted to each bar. They are never spotted in pairs and experts remain puzzled as to the possible existence of some Great Lifer Bar Patronage Schematic. These Hipsters possess also a chameleon like adaptability which allows them to complement the general atmosphere of their chosen environment. In the absence of a Lifer, many bars feel as incomplete as if, say, the jukebox blew a fuse. The Lifer is often resident historian of its terrain, able to recall the state of now-trendy environments during the dark days of pre-gentrification.

Social Function:

The Lifer knows everyone, but refrains from situations of prolonged intimacy. He either sits alone at the bar or floats randomly about, inserting himself fleetingly into the conversations of others [*see* below]. Only rarely have Lifers been observed actually arriving at or exiting from their preferred terrain. Seemingly, they are installed on a semipermanent basis.

Mental State:

It is safe to assume that many Lifers have suffered something of a break with reality at some point in their pasts. However, they are not completely insane; some experts have even hypothesized that this break is a consequence of choice. Many specimens profess mysterious and romantic pasts. Most have seen hard times, normally of the financial or romantic variety. The particulars of said backstories remain shrouded by a mist of alcohol-laced mumblings and esoterically delivered physical gestures. What remains clear is that they are survivors.

Interaction:

As noted above, The Lifer does occasionally step outside the bounds of his internal monologue in order to interact with those around him. *Remain calm.* While harmless, this Hipster's unusual verbal technique can be a bit disorienting and may create something of an Alice in Wonderlandy effect, as many Lifers are either quietly brilliant or borderline psychotic. Casual observers should steel themselves to a period of abstract, philosophical meanderings interspersed with liberal quantities of pithy soul searching.

By Day:

Appearances notwithstanding, Lifers are not total derelicts. In fact, many are secretly employed, often as Computer Programmers. Certain specimens may, therefore, exhibit professional lives, yet never social ones. Subject to no known nocturnal schedule or responsibility, The Lifer is always available.

Habitat:

Though they cut across most social boundaries, these Hipsters seem to have a penchant for rock and roll clubs or otherwise gritty and simplistic environs. Trendy lounges and upscale clubs remain outside of the species' normative terrain. Somewhat surprisingly, The Lifer does not stick to a particular seat or stool of choice, though this transience does little to hinder immediate identification.

In Boston, MA:

SILHOUETTE LOUNGE *(200 Brighton Avenue)*—". . . Who wouldn't miss it? I mean as much as you can miss something you never really had. I never asked them to cut it off, though, they just took it upon themselves. The fact that it's even legal is sort of puzzling, I think. I could like sex ten times more. It's okay now, but it might be like fireworks every time had they left me intact. That's why we don't talk. Well, there's more to it, but that's part . . ."

In Los Angeles, CA:

FROLIC ROOM *(6245 Hollywood Boulevard)*—". . . you gotta get it in season, after they're all fed and full, right? Fat. That venison meat is somethin' else, I'm tellin' ya. Sweet. We used to smoke it, after we took it home and cleaned it, just smoked it for like three days, put it on a roll. Mmm, a little gamy, but real nice. Hard to get out here, though. One day I'm gonna drive east, rent a truck or somethin', do Route 66 in reverse, you know? . . ."

In New York, NY:

MANITOBA'S *(99 Avenue B bet. 6th and 7th Streets)*—". . . so I feed him, right? because that's just what was done. There was no expectations or entitlement isn't what it is right now. We were all over every place, gettin' in little scraps or just, like, our hands dirty? I know now, but there wasn't any guarantee or any real method for remaining positive, it just went there somehow . . ."

WCOU RADIO [A.K.A "TILE BAR"] *(115 First Avenue at 7th Street)*— ". . . this is something that not a lot of people realize or even think about. I mean some might, but they're in the minority, which brings us right back around to where we started. You can't just walk through life, or the world here, with your head down, 'cause it's all shit, you know? Like Iggy said . . ."

Appendix I:
Recommended Field Gear
and Technique

It is imperative that the neophyte first acquaint himself with the full breadth of our Hipsters, an overview best achieved through perusal of any one of various Field Guides available on the subject, such as this one. Though it may prove possible to gain some cursory knowledge through simple bookstore browsing, both the observer's field results and the author's bank balance will improve significantly as a result of actual purchase.

The following main points should, if followed closely, serve the observer well regardless of Hipster being pursued:

1. **Dress**—It is suggested that before venturing into the field, the observer spend some time assembling an outfit which generally conforms to the intended target's aesthetic. Conveniently, most "countercultural" species are best approached while wearing one standard outfit: black, slightly beat-up shoes; worn, boot-cut, vintage-washed jeans; nondescript solid T-shirt; windbreaker-type jacket or hooded, zip-up sweatshirt (weather permitting).

2. **Gear**—Observers are urged to travel lightly. While some experts still insist on carrying about their person such traditional accoutrements as a compass, maps, weather charts, a teakettle, butterfly nets, insect repellent, *The Andy Warhol Diaries*, sketch tablets, canteens, dried fruits, suntan lotion, and a sextant, many modern field researchers have come to eschew these accessories in favor

of a simple notebook, a reliable pen, and a small pair of binoculars.

3. **Remain Still**—Hipsters are known to be easily startled and can sense fear or lack of comfort. Whenever possible, remain in the shadows or corner. Do not dance. Partake only in libations suited to your surroundings (ordering a double Mai Tai, for example, at a Biker Bar has been known to send up something of a red flag).

4. **Vision**—One should endeavor to fine-tune his or her peripheral vision, an activity best pursued on occasion of long and lonely dateless evenings.

5. **Listening**—Hipsters' speech patterns and mating calls have long been considered an exceptional source of comedy. One recent trip to the Astor Place Reserves in New York yielded this gem of resignation, delivered from one female specimen to another: "Well, a new skinny boy is a new skinny boy." Had the observer, in this case the author, been focused simply on their pert, coltish physiques, said dialogue would have no doubt passed unnoticed, much to the detriment of several subsequent cocktail-hour anecdotes.

These simple rules are designed to facilitate smooth transition from the sidelines to the field. By studying these tenets until they become second nature, even observers of questionable social skill should be able to conduct themselves, if not admirably, then at least reasonably while in pursuit of these spectacular creatures.

Appendix II: Approaching a Dangerous Hipster

Many are the overconfident observers who, thinking themselves invincible, are cut down in the midst of flirting with an Outlaw Biker's Old Lady or attending an Oi! concert having neglected to first remove their yarmulke. Professional Hipthologists consider funeral arrangements an integral, if unfortunate, aspect of their position, coming part and parcel with more joyous concerns, be it the annual Nose Ring Symposium in Honolulu or tracking the springtime migration of aging Boston AlternaGirls to Poconos-area waitressing positions.

The following Hipsters have been ruled "dangerous" as a whole by an internationally convened board of experts: **Outlaw Bikers, Black Metal Heads, Skinheads, Thugz, Straight-Edgers**, and **Butch Lesbians.**

These Hipsters may prove quite gluttonous. While on safari, observers are cautioned to keep food products in a location difficult for most specimens to breach, such as a "Grand Old Party" tote bag or Columbus Day Memorial coffee mug.

It is important to pay close attention to any sign of alarm caused by your presence. In addition, always approach these Hipsters from a downwind position, as your freshly scrubbed scent may alarm them. Remain intensely quiet and do not interfere; your intention should be to observe them in their natural state, without interference. Do not antagonize the Hipster in any way or force it to behave unnaturally for the benefit of photography. Thugz, in particular, do not enjoy being poked with sticks. Above all else, do not block the escape route of a Hipster who has grown skittish. Many seemingly aggressive specimens would rather flee than engage in violence.

The following points should be memorized by those venturing into hazardous terrain:

1. Take a moment to assess the situation before commencing approach.

2. Ascertain the precise number of Hipsters in the area before proceeding further. Large numbers are best avoided.

3. If possible, determine the mood of the Hipster. For example, Black Metal Heads fresh off a church arson may prove jovial and are thus ideal to approach.

4. Approach slowly following an indirect route.

5. Always plan a prospective exit path for yourself.

6. If the pack contains both males and females, determine if the Hipsters are mating. If so, specimens may prove exceptionally aggressive. Do not scope a Thug'z beeyatch.

7. Expect the unexpected. Even Butch Lesbians may grab your crotch.

Though the issue of safety is paramount, beginners need not be discouraged by the above. Most excursions into the field provide harmless, enjoyable recreation. Even where dangerous species are concerned, actual incidents of violence are statistically quite rare.

Acknowledgments

My deepest gratitude to everyone who helped me on this project. Had my advance been larger, I'd buy you all a drink.

Particular thanks needs be paid to Bill Griffith and Patrick O'Grady, who contributed more humor and detail than I'd like to admit. Someone needs to give these guys their own book deals, and fast. Amy DeCicco gave so much of herself to this book that I'm left practically speechless. Her patience, good taste, and unflagging enthusiasm meant more to me than I think she realizes. Without the generosity of Patricia Clarkson, I might have blown this before it even got started. Thank you. I wish I were older, or taller. Big ups also to Chris Naughton for his continued support and willingness to pay much more rent than I do. If it weren't for his Pfizer salary, I'd be living in an apartment behind Super Fresh by now.

This book is based on interviews, and in that regard many people went above and beyond anything I could have rightly expected. Mad props, especially, to Margo Tiffen and Holly von Heintz (née McKinley), who each provided an unbelievable wealth of information. Holly, I hate that you moved to Los Angeles. I also need to give a major shout out to my peeps Laura Reilly Bell, Heather Lynch, Julie Stefanov, Cheryl Burke, Krissy Schuchman, Jessica Kushner, Noah Kerner, Emily Oviatt, Peggy Tachdjian, Deepak Dadlani, Meghan Sutherland, Annick Rosenfield, Bettina Bilger, Delroy Binger, Rachel Hill, David Winn, Liz Wallman, Justine Day, Judi DeCicco, Steg von Heintz, Justine Day, Shani Ankori, Stefanie Aiello, John Clark, Jackie Endriss, Susan Leader, Michelle Stark, Shira Ankori, George Griffith, Teresa Reilly, Becky Shlapack, Susan's metal friends, John Adair, Beth Datlowe, Rodney Wiltshire, Kathy Lendle, Sabrina Rowe, Amelia Zalcman, and my two ex-neighbors from Watts Street. To those who are missing, it only means my computer crashed and along with it my "book thanks" file. Please forgive me.

My agent, Mike Harriot, took a chance on a rough idea and his confidence made all the difference. His support has helped me compete with my younger sister's burgeoning sales career at most family gatherings. Thanks, Mike. All struggling writers should besiege his office with phone calls immediately. Or better yet, just drop by.

A special thank you to Rebecca Cole, who is as good an editor as she is a hair model. I can only hope that this book brings her even more joy than that one she edited on wood stain, though I realize such a wish is lofty.

The owners of the Lakeside Lounge in New York graciously allowed us to take our authors' photo in their fine establishment. Stop in for Happy Hour. It's great.

Last, I need to thank my wonderfully supportive and highly amusing parents for never once pressuring me to attend medical school. I hope seeing this in the local bookstore makes them feel better about the fact that their twenty-seven-year-old son had to move back home for two months last summer. To my mother's repeated entreaties that I dedicate this to her, I can only say "maybe next time?" Seriously, though, they are the best, and much better than your parents.

Oh, one more thing: I'd like to pour a little out for the Hipsters who couldn't make it to the final draft. Perhaps we will all meet again one day in a revised edition. Preferably in hardcover.

© Annick Rosenfeld

About the Author and Illustrator

JOSH AIELLO cut his literary teeth writing scathing editorials for the school paper, most notably *J'accuse Janitor Carlson*, which earned him after-school detention for one week. He attended film school at Boston University, where his signature string of bad luck with women resulted in the production of several well-received short films. After graduation, Josh co-wrote and co-directed the feature film *Island*, which attracted some attention, mainly from his creditors and mother. He currently lives in Manhattan and wishes his bedroom were larger.

MATTHEW SHULTZ is a native Michigander living in New York City. A sucker for a pretty face, Matthew enjoys bicycle rides, macaroni and cheese, and ice hockey. He "studied" art at a small college in central Illinois, working summers as a pet caricaturist. In the years since, his drawings have appeared in any number of esoteric and obscure periodicals. He is not Jewish, and has no idea how that got started. Behind Matthew's disagreeable exterior, he can be quite compassionate and sincere.